Learn Khmer For Complete Beginners

Alma M. Park

All rights reserved. Copyright © 2023 Alma M. Park

COPYRIGHT © 2023 Alma M. Park

All rights reserved.

No part of this book must be reproduced, stored in a retrieval system, or shared by any means, electronic, mechanical, photocopying, recording, or otherwise, without written permission from the publisher.

Every precaution has been taken in the preparation of this book; still the publisher and author assume no responsibility for errors or omissions. Nor do they assume any liability for damages resulting from the use of the information contained herein.

Legal Notice:

This book is copyright protected and is only meant for your individual use. You are not allowed to amend, distribute, sell, use, quote or paraphrase any of its part without the written consent of the author or publisher.

Introduction

This is a comprehensive language guide that covers various aspects of the Khmer language, making it an ideal resource for those looking to start their journey in learning Khmer.

The guide introduces learners to essential greetings and survival phrases, enabling them to engage in basic conversations and navigate daily interactions effectively. It also covers the fundamentals of telling time in Khmer, providing learners with the tools to schedule and plan their activities.

Additionally, the guide delves into vocabulary related to family members and relationships, allowing learners to discuss their family and connect with Khmer-speaking individuals on a personal level. It also includes sections on body parts, months, days, seasons, shapes, and colors, providing a well-rounded foundation for language acquisition.

Learners interested in discussing food and dining experiences will find valuable vocabulary and phrases in the guide, making it easier to order food at restaurants and engage in culinary conversations. The guide also equips learners with travel-related terminology, helping them navigate transportation and accommodations during their journeys.

Furthermore, it explores various aspects of everyday life, such as shopping, emergencies, weather discussions, and more, providing a comprehensive overview of the Khmer language and culture. Whether you're a traveler, a language enthusiast, or simply interested in broadening your linguistic horizons, this book offers a valuable entry point into the Khmer language and its rich cultural context.

Contents

Greetings/Survival Phrases 1
Time 3
Shapes 4
Colors: 4
Numbers 5
Family: 8
Body Parts 9
Months, Days, Seasons 11
Clothes 13
Animals 20
Shopping 23
At the Restaurant 25
Travel 28
Dating Phrases 81

Greetings/Survival Phrases

Hi!- suosdei
Hi!- suosdei
Hello - Chom Reap Sour
Hello - Chom Reap Sour
Sir - lohk
Sir - lohk
Madam - lohk srei
Madam - lohk srei
Hello, sir. - johm ree·uhp soo·uh lohk
Hello, sir. - johm ree·uhp soo·uh lohk
Hello, Madam. - johm ree·uhp soo·uh lohk srei
Hello, Madam. - johm ree·uhp soo·uh lohk srei
Are you well? - sohk sa·baay jee·aa day
Are you well? - sohk sa·baay jee·aa day
Excuse me, I'm sorry. - sohm-đoh
Excuse me, I'm sorry. - sohm-đoh
Good morning! - arounsuosdei
Good morning! - arounsuosdei
Good afternoon! - tivea suosdei
Good afternoon! - tivea suosdei
Good evening! - sa y nd suosdei
Good evening! - sa y nd suosdei
Welcome! - saum svakom
Welcome! - saum svakom
How are you? (friendly) - tae eng sokhasabbay te?
How are you? (friendly) - tae eng sokhasabbay te?
How are you? (polite) - tae anak sokhasabbay te?
How are you? (polite) - tae anak sokhasabbay te?
I'm fine, thank you! - khnhom sokhasabbay cheate saum arkoun!
I'm fine, thank you! - khnhom sokhasabbay cheate saum arkoun!
And you? (friendly) - choheng vinh?
And you? (friendly) - choheng vinh?
What's up? - tae mean rueng avei?
What's up? - tae mean rueng avei?
And you? (polite) - choh anak vinh?
And you? (polite) - choh anak vinh?
Good - sokhasabbay
Good - sokhasabbay
Bad - minsokh sabbay
Bad - minsokh sabbay

Happy - sabbay
Happy - sabbay
Sad - kaettoukkh
Sad - kaettoukkh
Thank you! - saum arkoun!
Thank you! - saum arkoun!
Thank you very much! - saum arkoun chraen!
Thank you very much! - saum arkoun chraen!
You're welcome! - min ei te!
You're welcome! - min ei te!
Have a nice day! - saum aoy thngainih meante sechakdeisokh!
Have a nice day! - saum aoy thngainih meante sechakdeisokh!
Good night! - reatreisuosdei!
Good night! - reatreisuosdei!
See you later! - chuobaknea pelokraoy!
See you later! - chuobaknea pelokraoy!
Have a good trip! - saum thveudamnaer daoy sovotthephap!
Have a good trip! - saum thveudamnaer daoy sovotthephap!
It was nice talking to you! - rikreay del ban niyeay cheamuoy anak!
It was nice talking to you! - rikreay del ban niyeay cheamuoy anak!
Hey! Friend! - he! Samleanh!
Hey! Friend! - he! Samleanh!
Good night and sweet dreams! - reatrei suor stei ning so be nt la!
Good night and sweet dreams! - reatrei suor stei ning so be nt la!
Congratulations! - saum abaarsatr!
Congratulations! - saum abaarsatr!
Best wishes! - saumchounopr!
Best wishes! - saumchounopr!
until next time - rhautadl pelokraoy
until next time - rhautadl pelokraoy
My thoughts are with you - koumnit robsakhnhom ku now cheamuoy anak
My thoughts are with you - koumnit robsakhnhom ku now cheamuoy anak
Congrats to the newly engaged! - saum abaarsatr champoh anak del teub phcheab thmei!
Congrats to the newly engaged! - saum abaarsatr champoh anak del teub phcheab thmei!
Have fun! - saum rikreay!
Have fun! - saum rikreay!
lots of love! - sraleanh chraennasa!
lots of love! - sraleanh chraennasa!
Take care! - theroksaa!
Take care! - theroksaa!
With sympathy - daoy ktei anetasaur

With sympathy - daoy ktei anetasaur
My family name is… - chmuah dtra-goal…
My family name is… - chmuah dtra-goal…
I come from… - moak bpee…
I come from… - moak bpee…
Phnom Penh - p'noom bpeung
Phnom Penh - p'noom bpeung
English language - pee-a saa ong-klayh
English language - pee-a saa ong-klayh

Time

Time - Moung
Time - Moung
What time is it? - Moung bon maan?
What time is it? - Moung bon maan?
Minute - Natii
Minute - Natii
Day - T'ngai
Day - T'ngai
Week - Aa-dteut
Week - Aa-dteut
Year - Ch'nam
Year - Ch'nam
Yesterday - M'serl-meign
Yesterday - M'serl-meign
Tomorrow - Sa-aik
Tomorrow - Sa-aik
Last week - Aa-dteut moohn
Last week - Aa-dteut moohn
There are seven days in a week. - mean brapir thngai knong muoy sa bta .
There are seven days in a week. - mean brapir thngai knong muoy sa bta .
Today is Saturday, September 10th. - thngainih chea thngaisaw ti 10 khekanhnhea .
Today is Saturday, September 10th. - thngainih chea thngaisaw ti 10 khekanhnhea .
Tomorrow afternoon - rsiel thngaisaek
Tomorrow afternoon - rsiel thngaisaek
Three minutes - bei neati
Three minutes - bei neati
Shortly after - minyour bonman
Shortly after - minyour bonman
I've known her for a long time - khnhom skal neang tangpi yournasa mk haey
I've known her for a long time - khnhom skal neang tangpi yournasa mk haey
In about 2 years - knongorypel brahel 2 chhnam

In about 2 years - knongorypel brahel 2 chhnam
In about 2 months - knongorypel brahel 2 khe
In about 2 months - knongorypel brahel 2 khe
Just in time - kreante nowknong pelvelea
Just in time - kreante nowknong pelvelea

Shapes

Cylinder - saileang
Cylinder - saileang
Circle - rongvong
Circle - rongvong
Square - kare
Square - kare
Cube - koub
Cube - koub
Hexagon - chh kaon
Hexagon - chh kaon
Triangle - treikaon

Triangle - treikaon

Crescent - adthochan

Crescent - adthochan

Oval - reangopongokrapeu

Oval - reangopongokrapeu

Pentagon - montir banhchokaon

Pentagon - montir banhchokaon

Colors:

Black - khmaw
Black - khmaw
Blue - khiev
Blue - khiev
Brown - tnaot
Brown - tnaot
Gray - brapheh
Gray - brapheh
Green - baitng
Green - baitng
Orange - tukakrauch
Orange - tukakrauch
Red - krahm

Red - krahm
White - sa
White - sa
Yellow - lueng
Yellow - lueng
Dark color - pnr chasa
Dark color - pnr chasa
Light color - pnr khchei
Light color - pnr khchei
Colors - pnr
Colors - pnr
The sky is blue - mekh pnrkhiev
The sky is blue - mekh pnrkhiev
Your cat is white - chhmar robsa an k pnrsa
Your cat is white - chhmar robsa an k pnrsa
Black is his favorite color - pnrkhmaw chea pnr del keat penhchett cheangke
Black is his favorite color - pnrkhmaw chea pnr del keat penhchett cheangke
Red is not his favorite color - pnr krahm minmen chea pnr del keat chaulchett te
Red is not his favorite color - pnr krahm minmen chea pnr del keat chaulchett te
She drives a yellow car - neang baek lan pnrlueng
She drives a yellow car - neang baek lan pnrlueng
I have black hair - khnhom mean sak pnrkhmaw
I have black hair - khnhom mean sak pnrkhmaw

Numbers

One - muoy
One - muoy
Two - pir
Two - pir
Three - bei
Three - bei
Four - buon
Four - buon
Five - bram
Five - bram
Six - bram muo uo y
Six - bram muo uo y
Seven - brapir
Seven - brapir
Eight - brabei
Eight - brabei
Nine - brabuon
Nine - brabuon

Ten - db
Ten - db
Eleven - db muo uo y
Eleven - db muo uo y
Twelve - dbpir
Twelve - dbpir
Thirteen - db bei
Thirteen - db bei
Fourteen - db buon
Fourteen - db buon
Fifteen - dbbram
Fifteen - dbbram
Sixteen - dbbra muoy
Sixteen - dbbra muoy
Seventeen - dbbra pir
Seventeen - dbbra pir
Eighteen - dbbra bei
Eighteen - dbbra bei
Nineteen - dbbra buon
Nineteen - dbbra buon
Twenty - mphei
Twenty - mphei
Thirty - samseb
Thirty - samseb
Forty - seseb
Forty - seseb
Fifty - haseb
Fifty - haseb
Sixty - hokseb
Sixty - hokseb
Seventy - chetseb
Seventy - chetseb
Eighty - betseb
Eighty - betseb
Ninety - kawseb
Ninety - kawseb
One hundred - muoy ry
One hundred - muoy ry
One thousand - muoy pean
One thousand - muoy pean
Five thousand - Pram-pin
Five thousand - Pram-pin
Ten thousand - Muoy-meun

Ten thousand - Muoy-meun
One million - muoy lean
One million - muoy lean
I'm thirty years old - khnhom ayou samseb chhnam
I'm thirty years old - khnhom ayou samseb chhnam
First - timuoy
First - timuoy
Second - tipir
Second - tipir
Third - tibei
Third - tibei
Fourth - ti buon
Fourth - ti buon
Fifth - ti bram
Fifth - ti bram
Sixth - ti bram muo uo y
Sixth - ti bram muo uo y
Seventh - ti brapir
Seventh - ti brapir
Eighth - ti brabei
Eighth - ti brabei
Ninth - ti bram buo n
Ninth - ti bram buo n
Tenth - ti db
Tenth - ti db
Eleventh - ti dbmuoy
Eleventh - ti dbmuoy
Twelfth - ti dbpir
Twelfth - ti dbpir
Thirteenth - ti db bei
Thirteenth - ti db bei
Fourteenth - ti db buon
Fourteenth - ti db buon
Fifteenth - ti dbbram
Fifteenth - ti dbbram
Sixteenth - ti dbbra muoy
Sixteenth - ti dbbra muoy
Seventeenth - ti dbbra pir
Seventeenth - ti dbbra pir
Eighteenth - ti dbbra bei
Eighteenth - ti dbbra bei
Nineteenth - ti dbbra buon
Nineteenth - ti dbbra buon

Twentieth - ti mphei
Twentieth - ti mphei
Once - mtong
Once - mtong
Twice - pir dng
Twice - pir dng

Family:

Daughter - kaunosrei
Daughter - kaunosrei
Son - kaunobrosa
Son - kaunobrosa
Sister - bangosrei / baaunosrei
Sister - bangosrei / baaunosrei
Brother - bangobrosa / baaunobrosa
Brother - bangobrosa / baaunobrosa
Baby - teark
Baby - teark
Child (male) - kmeng(brosa)
Child (male) - kmeng(brosa)
Child (f) - kmeng(srei)
Child (f) - kmeng(srei)
Father - aupouk
Father - aupouk
Mother - mteay
Mother - mteay
Husband - btei / svami
Husband - btei / svami
Wife - phriyea / braponth
Wife - phriyea / braponth
Cousin (m) - bangobaaun chidaun muo uo y(brosa)
Cousin (m) - bangobaaun chidaun muo uo y(brosa)
Cousin (f) - bangobaaun chidaun muo uo y(srei)
Cousin (f) - bangobaaun chidaun muo uo y(srei)
Aunt - ming
Aunt - ming
Nephew - kmuoyobrosa
Nephew - kmuoyobrosa
Boy - ke m ng brosa
Boy - ke m ng brosa
Grandmother - chidaun
Grandmother - chidaun

Woman - strei
Woman - strei
Uncle - pou
Uncle - pou
Grandfather - chitea
Grandfather - chitea
Niece - kmuoyosrei
Niece - kmuoyosrei
Man - borsa
Man - borsa
Girl - ke m ng srei
Girl - ke m ng srei
People - brachapolorodth / brachachn
People - brachapolorodth / brachachn
Sister-in-law - bangothlai srei
Sister-in-law - bangothlai srei
Brother-in-law - bangothlai
Brother-in-law - bangothlai
Mother-in-law - mdeayokmek
Mother-in-law - mdeayokmek
Father-in-law - aupoukakmek
Father-in-law - aupoukakmek
Son-in-law - kaunobrasaea r bros
Son-in-law - kaunobrasaea r bros
What's your brother called? - tae ke haw bng / baaunobrosa robsa anak tha dauchamdech?
What's your brother called? - tae ke haw bng / baaunobrosa robsa anak tha dauchamdech?
Where does your father work? - tae au pouk robsa anak thveukear now kanlengna?
Where does your father work? - tae au pouk robsa anak thveukear now kanlengna?
I love my husband - khnhom sralanh bdei robsakhnhom
I love my husband - khnhom sralanh bdei robsakhnhom
How old is your sister? - tae bng / baaunosrei robsa anak mean ayou bonman?
How old is your sister? - tae bng / baaunosrei robsa anak mean ayou bonman?
Your daughter is very cute - kaunosrei robsa anak saat nasa
Your daughter is very cute - kaunosrei robsa anak saat nasa
This is my wife - nih chea braponth robsakhnhom
This is my wife - nih chea braponth robsakhnhom

Body Parts

Mouth - meat
Mouth - meat

Nose - chramouh
Nose - chramouh
Tongue - a nta t
Tongue - a nta t
Teeth - thmenh
Teeth - thmenh
Ear - trachiek
Ear - trachiek
Eye - phnek
Eye - phnek
Face - moukh
Face - moukh
Head - kbal
Head - kbal
Neck - k
Neck - k
Arm - dai
Arm - dai
Shoulder - sma
Shoulder - sma
Chest - troung
Chest - troung
Back - khnang
Back - khnang
Fingers - mreamdai
Fingers - mreamdai
Feet - cheung
Feet - cheung
Hair - sak
Hair - sak
Hand - dai
Hand - dai
Heart - behdaung
Heart - behdaung
Leg - cheung
Leg - cheung
Stomach - poh
Stomach - poh
Chin - chhi n
Chin - chhi n
Hip - trakak
Hip - trakak
Eyebrow - romchenhcheum

Eyebrow - romchenhcheum
Brain - khuorokbal
Brain - khuorokbal
Waist - changkih
Waist - changkih
Elbow - kengdai
Elbow - kengdai
Bone - chhaoeng
Bone - chhaoeng
Liver - thlaem
Liver - thlaem
Muscle - sachdom
Muscle - sachdom
Eyelash - romophnek
Eyelash - romophnek
She has beautiful eyes - neang mean phnek srasa saat
She has beautiful eyes - neang mean phnek srasa saat
We see with our eyes - yeung meulkheunh daoysaar phnek teangpir robsa yeung
We see with our eyes - yeung meulkheunh daoysaar phnek teangpir robsa yeung
He feels with his hand - keat bah daoy brae dai robsa keat
He feels with his hand - keat bah daoy brae dai robsa keat
You hear with your ears - anak sdab lu daoysaar trachiek teangpir robsa anak
You hear with your ears - anak sdab lu daoysaar trachiek teangpir robsa anak
I smell with my nose - khnhom thoumklen daoysaar chramouh robsakhnhom
I smell with my nose - khnhom thoumklen daoysaar chramouh robsakhnhom
She tastes with her tongue - neang doeng rosacheate daoysaar andat robsa neang
She tastes with her tongue - neang doeng rosacheate daoysaar andat robsa neang

Months, Days, Seasons

Days - thngai
Days - thngai
Monday - chnt
Monday - chnt
Tuesday - angkea
Tuesday - angkea
Wednesday - pouth
Wednesday - pouth
Thursday - pr h ssa
Thursday - pr h ssa
Friday - sokr
Friday - sokr
Saturday - saw

Saturday - saw
Sunday - atity
Sunday - atity
January - mokrea
January - mokrea
February - komph
February - komph
March - minea
March - minea
April - mesaea
April - mesaea
May - usaphea
May - usaphea
June - mithona
June - mithona
July - kakkada
July - kakkada
August - seiha
August - seiha
September - kanhnhea
September - kanhnhea
October - tola
October - tola
November - vichchheka
November - vichchheka
December - thnou
December - thnou
Autumn - sarotordauv
Autumn - sarotordauv
Winter - seserordauv
Winter - seserordauv
Spring - niteakhordauv
Spring - niteakhordauv
Summer - kimhordauv
Summer - kimhordauv
Seasons - rdauv
Seasons - rdauv
Months - khe
Months - khe
Time - pelvelea
Time - pelvelea
Hour - maong
Hour - maong

Minute - neati
Minute - neati
Second - vineati
Second - vineati
Last Year - ch'nam moon
Last Year - ch'nam moon
New Year - ch'nam thmey
New Year - ch'nam thmey
Next Year - ch'nam groy
Next Year - ch'nam groy
Morning - pruk
Morning - pruk
Evening - ingeach
Evening - ingeach
Night - yb
Night - yb
Midnight - athreat
Midnight - athreat
Yesterday was Sunday - msailminh chea thngaiaeatity
Yesterday was Sunday - msailminh chea thngaiaeatity
Today is Monday - thngainih chea thngaichnt
Today is Monday - thngainih chea thngaichnt
See you tomorrow! - chuobaknea thngaisaek!
See you tomorrow! - chuobaknea thngaisaek!
I will visit you in August - khnhom nung tow leng anak now kheseiha
I will visit you in August - khnhom nung tow leng anak now kheseiha
Winter is very cold here - seserordauv ku trachak khlang nasa now tinih
Winter is very cold here - seserordauv ku trachak khlang nasa now tinih
I was born in July - khnhom kaet now khekakkada
I was born in July - khnhom kaet now khekakkada

Clothes

Coat - avthom kraw
Coat - avthom kraw
Dress - saamliekbampeak
Dress - saamliekbampeak
Hat - muok
Hat - muok
Jacket - avthom daikhlei
Jacket - avthom daikhlei
Pants - khaocheungveng
Pants - khaocheungveng

Shirt - avyut daikhlei
Shirt - avyut daikhlei
Shoes - sbekcheung
Shoes - sbekcheung
Socks - sraomcheung
Socks - sraomcheung
Underwear - khaotrnab
Underwear - khaotrnab
Sweater - avyut
Sweater - avyut
Suit - av chhout
Suit - av chhout
Tie - kraveatk
Tie - kraveatk
Belt - khsae kr veat
Belt - khsae kr veat
Gloves - sraomdai
Gloves - sraomdai
Umbrella - chhtr
Umbrella - chhtr
Wallet - kabaub daklouy borsa
Wallet - kabaub daklouy borsa
Watch - nealekadai
Watch - nealekadai
Glasses - venta
Glasses - venta
Ring - chenhchien
Ring - chenhchien
Clothes - saamliekbampeak
Clothes - saamliekbampeak
Cotton - kabbas
Cotton - kabbas
Swimsuit - chhout heltuk
Swimsuit - chhout heltuk
Blouse - av
Blouse - av
Scarf - kr mea
Scarf - kr mea
Apron - a pho n
Apron - a pho n
Leather - sbek
Leather - sbek
These shoes are small - sbekcheung teangnih tauch

These shoes are small - sbekcheung teangnih tauch
These pants are long - khao teangnih mean cheungveng
These pants are long - khao teangnih mean cheungveng
I lost my socks - khnhom ban chrouh bat sraomcheung
I lost my socks - khnhom ban chrouh bat sraomcheung
Do you like my dress? - tae anak chaulchett saamliekbampeak robsakhnhom te?
Do you like my dress? - tae anak chaulchett saamliekbampeak robsakhnhom te?
She has a beautiful ring - neang mean chenhchien da saat
She has a beautiful ring - neang mean chenhchien da saat
It looks good on you - vea meul tow samnung anak
It looks good on you - vea meul tow samnung anak

Food

Milk - tuk daoh ko
Milk - tuk daoh ko
Butter - br
Butter - br
Cheese - brahok barang
Cheese - brahok barang
Bread - nombng
Bread - nombng
Meal - ahar
Meal - ahar
Breakfast - ahar pelopruk
Breakfast - ahar pelopruk
Lunch - ahar thngaitrang
Lunch - ahar thngaitrang
Dinner - ahar pelolngeach
Dinner - ahar pelolngeach
Salad - salat
Salad - salat
Sugar - skar
Sugar - skar
Salt - ambel
Salt - ambel
Orange juice - tukakrauch
Orange juice - tukakrauch
Soda - tuksauda(dauch kaukakaula)
Soda - tuksauda(dauch kaukakaula)
Coffee - kahve
Coffee - kahve
Tea - tukte
Tea - tukte

Fish - sach trei
Fish - sach trei
Meat - sach
Meat - sach
Chicken - sach mean
Chicken - sach mean
Pizza - nom phi hsaa
Pizza - nom phi hsaa
Eggs - saout
Eggs - saout
Sandwich - nombng sang vich
Sandwich - nombng sang vich
Ice cream - karem
Ice cream - karem
Water - tuk
Water - tuk
Food - mhoubaeahar
Food - mhoubaeahar
Lemons - phlekrauch chhmar
Lemons - phlekrauch chhmar
Apples - phle baom
Apples - phle baom
Oranges - phlekrauch
Oranges - phlekrauch
Peaches - phle be sa
Peaches - phle be sa
Figs - phle lvea
Figs - phle lvea
Pears - phle pr
Pears - phle pr
Pineapples - phle mneasa
Pineapples - phle mneasa
Grapes - phle tompeangbaychour
Grapes - phle tompeangbaychour
Strawberries - phle st r beu ri
Strawberries - phle st r beu ri
Bananas - phle chek
Bananas - phle chek
Watermelon - phle au loek
Watermelon - phle au loek
Avocados - phle a vou kadau
Avocados - phle a vou kadau
Carrots - karot

Carrots - karot
Corn - pot
Corn - pot
Cucumbers - trasak
Cucumbers - trasak
Garlic - khtoemsa
Garlic - khtoemsa
Lettuce - spaisa
Lettuce - spaisa
Olives - au liv
Olives - au liv
Onions - khtoembareang
Onions - khtoembareang
Peppers - mrech
Peppers - mrech
Potatoes - damlaung
Potatoes - damlaung
Pumpkin - lpow
Pumpkin - lpow
Beans - sandek
Beans - sandek
Tomatoes - bengbaoh
Tomatoes - bengbaoh
Spicy - hel
Spicy - hel
Chopsticks - jong-geh
Chopsticks - jong-geh
Knife - gam-bet
Knife - gam-bet
Spoon - slaab-bpria
Spoon - slaab-bpria
Fork - seom
Fork - seom
Oil - breng
Oil - breng
Sour - chour
Sour - chour
Basil - Basil
Basil - Basil
Meatball - sach bal
Meatball - sach bal
Almonds - a l mong
Almonds - a l mong

Bitter - chourocht
Bitter - chourocht
Cranberry - khatna ri
Cranberry - khatna ri
Broccoli - phka khatna khiev
Broccoli - phka khatna khiev
Zucchini - hsao k chhi ni
Zucchini - hsao k chhi ni
Pumpkin - lpow
Pumpkin - lpow
Beer - srabie r
Beer - srabie r
Seasoning - rdauv
Seasoning - rdauv
Roast - ang
Roast - ang
Frozen - k k
Frozen - k k
Chop - chrabeach
Chop - chrabeach
Raw - chaw
Raw - chaw
Melted - ban rleay
Melted - ban rleay
Poached - bramanh
Poached - bramanh
Squeeze - chrabeach
Squeeze - chrabeach
Fry - chien
Fry - chien
Grated - doengkoun
Grated - doengkoun
Recipe - roubamon
Recipe - roubamon
Boiled - chhaen
Boiled - chhaen
Recipe book - sievphow roubamon
Recipe book - sievphow roubamon
Bake - dot
Bake - dot
Ingredient - kruengophsaam
Ingredient - kruengophsaam
Flavor - rosacheate

Flavor - rosacheate
Rice - Bai
Rice - Bai
What food are you cooking? - Twer mahok ay?
What food are you cooking? - Twer mahok ay?

I'm full - Kynom cha-aet howie
I'm full - Kynom cha-aet howie
I like to eat all khmer food. - Khnom jol jet nam mhoob khmer dtiang os.
I like to eat all khmer food. - Khnom jol jet nam mhoob khmer dtiang os.
This fruit is delicious - phlechheu nih chhnganh
This fruit is delicious - phlechheu nih chhnganh
Vegetables are healthy - banle thveuaoy mean sokhpheap la
Vegetables are healthy - banle thveuaoy mean sokhpheap la
I like bananas - khnhom chaulchett nhoam phle chek
I like bananas - khnhom chaulchett nhoam phle chek
I don't like cucumber - khnhom min chaulchett nhoam phle trasak te
I don't like cucumber - khnhom min chaulchett nhoam phle trasak te
Bananas taste sweet - phle chek mean rosacheate phaem
Bananas taste sweet - phle chek mean rosacheate phaem
Lemons taste sour - phle krauchachhmar mean rosacheate chour
Lemons taste sour - phle krauchachhmar mean rosacheate chour
I'm hungry - khnhom khlean
I'm hungry - khnhom khlean
Do you have a bottle of water? - tae anak mean tuk muoy db te?
Do you have a bottle of water? - tae anak mean tuk muoy db te?
What kind of food do you like? - tae anak chaulchett ahar beb na?
What kind of food do you like? - tae anak chaulchett ahar beb na?
Are you thirsty? - tae anak srektuk te?
Are you thirsty? - tae anak srektuk te?
Breakfast is ready - ahar pelopruk riebcham ruochhaey
Breakfast is ready - ahar pelopruk riebcham ruochhaey
I like cheese - khnhom chaulchett brahok barang
I like cheese - khnhom chaulchett brahok barang
What food are you cooking? - Twer mahok ay?
What food are you cooking? - Twer mahok ay?
Would you like some tea? - lohk ɖrow-gaa ɖuhk-ɖai ɖay?
Would you like some tea? - lohk ɖrow-gaa ɖuhk-ɖai ɖay?
No, I want a glass of coffee. - baat-ɖay, kuh·nyohm ɖrow-gaa gaa·fay muy gaiw
No, I want a glass of coffee. - baat-ɖay, kuh·nyohm ɖrow-gaa gaa·fay muy gaiw
How much is it? - tuh·lai ƃohn·maan
How much is it? - tuh·lai ƃohn·maan
to have a meal - nyam-baay
to have a meal - nyam-baay

Here you are. - nih lohk
Here you are. - nih lohk
What is good today? - tae mean avei la now thngainih?
What is good today? - tae mean avei la now thngainih?
Thank you. Please bring me a... - saum arkoun . saum noam khnhom mok
Thank you. Please bring me a... - saum arkoun . saum noam khnhom mok
bottle of cold beer. - db srabie r trachak .
bottle of cold beer. - db srabie r trachak .
a bottle of drinking water. - db tukphoek .
a cup of tea. - temuoy peng .
a cup of tea. - temuoy peng .
I need a receipt. - khnhom trauvkar bangkeandai .
I need a receipt. - khnhom trauvkar bangkeandai .
I don't eat meat. - khnhom min briphok sach te .
I don't eat meat. - khnhom min briphok sach te .
How much per kilo? - tae knong muoy kilau thlai bonman?
How much per kilo? - tae knong muoy kilau thlai bonman?
How many kilo's do you need? - tae anak trauvkar bonman kilau?
How many kilo's do you need? - tae anak trauvkar bonman kilau?
Give me two kilos of… - aoy khnhom pir kilau...
Give me two kilos of… - aoy khnhom pir kilau...
Sorry. We have no beef. - somtosa . yeung kmean sachko te .
Sorry. We have no beef. - somtosa . yeung kmean sachko te .
Check, please! - <u>keut luy</u>
Check, please! - <u>keut luy</u>

Animals

Bird - satvasleab
Bird - satvasleab
Cat - chhma
Cat - chhma
Cow - konhi
Cow - konhi
Dog - chhke
Dog - chhke
Donkey - satv lea
Donkey - satv lea
Eagle - satv i nrti
Eagle - satv i nrti
Elephant - damri
Elephant - damri
Goat - ppe

Goat - ppe
Horse - seh
Horse - seh
Lion - tao
Lion - tao
Monkey - satv sva
Monkey - satv sva
Mouse - k ntor
Mouse - k ntor
Rabbit - tonsaeay
Rabbit - tonsaeay
Snake - psa
Snake - psa
Tiger - khla
Tiger - khla
Sheep - satv chiem
Sheep - satv chiem
Spider - pingpeang
Spider - pingpeang
Insect - satvalait
Insect - satvalait
Mosquito - mousa
Mosquito - mousa
Butterfly - meambaw
Butterfly - meambaw
Bear - khlakhmoum
Bear - khlakhmoum
Fish - dtrey
Fish - dtrey
Elephant - dom-rey
Elephant - dom-rey
Crocodile - grey-bpee
Crocodile - grey-bpee
water buffalo - grey-bey
water buffalo - grey-bey
Wolf - chgae-jo-jook
Wolf - chgae-jo-jook
Animal - satvapahn
Animal - satvapahn
Bee - satv khmoum
Bee - satv khmoum
Eagle - intri
Eagle - intri

Squirrel - kambrok
Squirrel - kambrok
Wasp - kaksaamnl
Wasp - kaksaamnl
Owl - satv titouy
Owl - satv titouy
Donkey - satv lea
Donkey - satv lea
Squid - muk
Squid - muk
Flamingo - hv lou mi nau
Flamingo - hv lou mi nau
Cockroach - satv kanleat
Cockroach - satv kanleat
Dolphin - phsaaot
Dolphin - phsaaot
Jaguar - cha hka r
Jaguar - cha hka r
Giraffe - hkei rea h
Giraffe - hkei rea h
Lizard - anak chomnuoy kar
Lizard - anak chomnuoy kar
Lobster - bangkong
Lobster - bangkong
Walrus - Walrus
Walrus - Walrus
Penguin - phe n khvi n
Penguin - phe n khvi n
Farm - ksedthan
Farm - ksedthan
Forest - prei
Forest - prei
water buffalo - krabei tuk
water buffalo - krabei tuk
Mosquito - mous
Mosquito - mous
I have a dog - khnhom mean chhke muoy kbal
I have a dog - khnhom mean chhke muoy kbal
She likes cats - khnhom chaulchett chhma
She likes cats - khnhom chaulchett chhma
Tigers are fast - satv khla rtluen
Tigers are fast - satv khla rtluen
Monkeys are funny - sva chea satv kr me chakr meum

Monkeys are funny - sva chea satv kr me chakr meum
Do you have any animals? - tae anak mean chenhchumosatv te?
Do you have any animals? - tae anak mean chenhchumosatv te?
Do you sell dog food? - tae anak mean lk ahar chhke te?
Do you sell dog food? - tae anak mean lk ahar chhke te?

Shopping

Expensive - thlai
Expensive - thlai
Cheap - thaok
Cheap - thaok
Cafe - kahve
Cafe - kahve
Cinema - rongkon
Cinema - rongkon
Supermarket - phsaar tomneub
Supermarket - phsaar tomneub
Gas station - sthaniy sang
Gas station - sthaniy sang
Museum - saromontir
Museum - saromontir
Pharmacy - au sa th sthan
Pharmacy - au sa th sthan
Credit card - bnnintean
Credit card - bnnintean
Cash - louy sotth
Cash - louy sotth
Check - sek
Check - sek
Parking - chamnt rth y nd
Parking - chamnt rth y nd
Butcher - kheatakar
Butcher - kheatakar
Coffee shop - hang kahve
Coffee shop - hang kahve
Bookshop - bannakar
Bookshop - bannakar
Supermarket - phsaar tomneub
Supermarket - phsaar tomneub
How much is this? - tae vea thlai bonman?
How much is this? - tae vea thlai bonman?
Can you take less? - tae ach chohthlai bantich ban te?

Can you take less? - tae ach chohthlai bantich ban te?
I'm just looking - khnhom kreante daer meul bonnaoh
I'm just looking - khnhom kreante daer meul bonnaoh
This is too expensive - vea thlai nasa
This is too expensive - vea thlai nasa
Do you accept credit cards? - tae anak ttuol yk b nd intean te?
Do you accept credit cards? - tae anak ttuol yk b nd intean te?
Only cash please! - yk te louy sotth bonnaoh!
Only cash please! - yk te louy sotth bonnaoh!
uncooked (husked) rice - ang·kaar
uncooked (husked) rice - ang·kaar
Kilogram - kee·low
Kilogram - kee·low
I have to buy two kilos of rice - kuh·nyom ɖrow ɖeen ang·kaar ƀee kee·low
I have to buy two kilos of rice - kuh·nyom ɖrow ɖeen ang·kaar ƀee kee·low
I just came to amuse myself - kuh·nyom kroun·ɖai mao daar·laing ɖay
I just came to amuse myself - kuh·nyom kroun·ɖai mao daar·laing ɖay
There are a lot of people at this market. - Neuw puh·saa nih mee·uhn mer·noo juh·rarn nah
There are a lot of people at this market. - Neuw puh·saa nih mee·uhn mer·noo juh·rarn nah
Here's a place selling fruit - nih gon·laayng lo·ak plai-cher
Here's a place selling fruit - nih gon·laayng lo·ak plai-cher
These oranges are very small. - krow·iht nih ɖow·iht-ɖow·iht nah
These oranges are very small. - krow·iht nih ɖow·iht-ɖow·iht nah
But these oranges are large and pretty too. - ɖai krow·iht nih tohm hao·y luh·aw pawng
But these oranges are large and pretty too. - ɖai krow·iht nih tohm hao·y luh·aw pawng
How much are these big oranges per dozen? - krow·iht tohm-tohm nih mu·low tuh·lai ƀohn·maan
How much are these big oranges per dozen? - krow·iht tohm-tohm nih mu·low tuh·lai ƀohn·maan
Those oranges are twenty-two riels per dozen. - krow·iht nooh mu·low tuh·lai muh·pei-ƀee riel
Those oranges are twenty-two riels per dozen. - krow·iht nooh mu·low tuh·lai muh·pei-ƀee riel
How many do you want? - lohk ɖrow-gaa ƀohn·maan
How many do you want? - lohk ɖrow-gaa ƀohn·maan
I want only a half-dozen. - kuh·nyom ɖrow-gaa ɖai gohn·lah low ɖay
I want only a half-dozen. - kuh·nyom ɖrow-gaa ɖai gohn·lah low ɖay
Are these bananas ripe yet? - jayk nih ɖum hao·y-roo-neuw?
Are these bananas ripe yet? - jayk nih ɖum hao·y-roo-neuw?
Those bananas aren't ripe yet. - jayk nooh muhn-ɖoan ɖum ɖay
Those bananas aren't ripe yet. - jayk nooh muhn-ɖoan ɖum ɖay

I'll take these two ripe bunches. - kuh·nyom yohk jayk đum ɓee snut nih
I'll take these two ripe bunches. - kuh·nyom yohk jayk đum ɓee snut nih
i never go to the old market because it is far from my house. - knhom min del tov phsar chas bpi- bpruah vea nov chngay pi pteah ro-bos knhom
i never go to the old market because it is far from my house. - knhom min del tov phsar chas bpi- bpruah vea nov chngay pi pteah ro-bos knhom

At the Restaurant

pork and rice - Bai sach chrouk
pork and rice - Bai sach chrouk
fried crab - Kdam chaa
fried crab - Kdam chaa
grilled squid - Ang dtray-meuk
grilled squid - Ang dtray-meuk
Spicy - hoer
Spicy - hoer
Sweet - phaem
Sweet - phaem
Salty - brai
Salty - brai
Plate - chan
Plate - chan
Fork - sam
Fork - sam
Knife - kabet
Knife - kabet
Spoon - slabaprea
Spoon - slabaprea
Table - to
Table - to
Menu - meunouy
Menu - meunouy
Food - mhoubaeahar
Food - mhoubaeahar
Dessert - bangaem
Dessert - bangaem
Water - tuk
Water - tuk
A cup of - muoy peng
A cup of - muoy peng
A glass of - muo uo ykev

A glass of - muo uo ykev
Salad - salad la
Salad - salad la
Soup - saoub
Soup - saoub
Bread - nombng
Bread - nombng
Black pepper - mrechakhmaw
Black pepper - mrechakhmaw
Salt - ambel
Salt - ambel
Tip - braktukte(louy samreab aoy anakabamreu)
Tip - braktukte(louy samreab aoy anakabamreu)
Napkin - kansaeng
Napkin - kansaeng
Sea food - Grueung samut
Sea food - Grueung samut
Peanuts - Sandek Dey
Peanuts - Sandek Dey
Gluten - Gluten
Gluten - Gluten
Beer - Bier
Beer - Bier
Wine - Sraa
Wine - Sraa
i am hungry - khnhom khlean
i am hungry - khnhom khlean
one water, please - saum muoy tuk
one water, please - saum muoy tuk
one beer, please - saum srabie r muoy kev
one beer, please - saum srabie r muoy kev
Where is there a good restaurant? - tae mean phochniyodthan del la te?
Where is there a good restaurant? - tae mean phochniyodthan del la te?
I'm vegetarian - khnhom min nhoam sach te
I'm vegetarian - khnhom min nhoam sach te
What's the name of this dish? - tae moukhamhoub nih chhmoh avei?
What's the name of this dish? - tae moukhamhoub nih chhmoh avei?
Waiter / waitress! - anakabamreu brosa / anakabamreu srei!
Waiter / waitress! - anakabamreu brosa / anakabamreu srei!
May we have the check please? - tae puok yeung ach som meul banhchi reay moukhamhoub ban te?
May we have the check please? - tae puok yeung ach som meul banhchi reay moukhamhoub ban te?

It is very delicious! - vea chhnganh nasa!
It is very delicious! - vea chhnganh nasa!
What do you recommend? - tae mhoub moukh na del anak kitthea chhnganh?(nhea)
What do you recommend? - tae mhoub moukh na del anak kitthea chhnganh?(nhea)
The bill please! - saum kitlouy!
The bill please! - saum kitlouy!
A glass of mineral water, please - saum kev tukre muoy kev
A glass of mineral water, please - saum kev tukre muoy kev
Do you have a table for two? - tae anak mean to samreab pir te?
Do you have a table for two? - tae anak mean to samreab pir te?
Is the sauce spicy? - tae tukachrolk mean rosacheate he r mente?
Is the sauce spicy? - tae tukachrolk mean rosacheate he r mente?
What can you recommend? - tae anak ach nenam aveikhleah?
What can you recommend? - tae anak ach nenam aveikhleah?
I would like to pay, please - khnhom chng bngbrak
I would like to pay, please - khnhom chng bngbrak
With ice - cheamuoy tukakak
With ice - cheamuoy tukakak
Without ice - bae kmean tukakak
Without ice - bae kmean tukakak
What light beers do you have? - tae anak mean srabie r sral aveikhleah?
What light beers do you have? - tae anak mean srabie r sral aveikhleah?
What dark beers do you have? - tae srabie r ngngut aveikhleah?
What dark beers do you have? - tae srabie r ngngut aveikhleah?
Keep the change. - touk brak ab nih choh .
Keep the change. - touk brak ab nih choh .
A table for four - to samreab buon
A table for four - to samreab buon
Could I have the dessert menu? - tae khnhom ach mean moukhamhoub bangaem ban te?
Could I have the dessert menu? - tae khnhom ach mean moukhamhoub bangaem ban te?
No, we don't have a reservation - te yeung min meankar kk te
No, we don't have a reservation - te yeung min meankar kk te
I'd like to make a reservation. - khnhom chng thveukear kk .
I'd like to make a reservation. - khnhom chng thveukear kk .
Are you open yet? - tae anak baek haey ryy now?
Are you open yet? - tae anak baek haey ryy now?
Can we sit over there? - tae yeung ach angkouy now tinoh ban te?
Can we sit over there? - tae yeung ach angkouy now tinoh ban te?
It was delicious - vea chhnganh nasa
It was delicious - vea chhnganh nasa
One more, please. - saum muoy banthem tiet .

One more, please. - saum muoy banthem tiet .
Enjoy your meal! - rikreay cheamuoy ahar robsa anak!
Enjoy your meal! - rikreay cheamuoy ahar robsa anak!
Let's eat! - taoh nhea!
Let's eat! - taoh nhea!
Pass the salt - hoch ambel
Pass the salt - hoch ambel
Can I have a taste? - tae khnhom ach mean rosacheate te?
Can I have a taste? - tae khnhom ach mean rosacheate te?
Excuse me, can we have the menu? - saumoaphytosa tae yeung ach mean moukhamhoub ban te?
Excuse me, can we have the menu? - saumoaphytosa tae yeung ach mean moukhamhoub ban te?
A glass of red wine. - srakrahm muoy kev .
A glass of red wine. - srakrahm muoy kev .
And what would you like to drink? - haey tae anak chng phoek avei?
And what would you like to drink? - haey tae anak chng phoek avei?
Can we have breakfast? - tae yeung ach nhoam ahar pelopruk ban te?
Can we have breakfast? - tae yeung ach nhoam ahar pelopruk ban te?
More bread, please - saum nombong banthem tiet
More bread, please - saum nombong banthem tiet
That's enough, thanks - krobkrean haey saum arkoun
That's enough, thanks - krobkrean haey saum arkoun
I am hungry. Is there a restaurant? - khnhom khlean . tae mean phochniyodthan te?
I am hungry. Is there a restaurant? - khnhom khlean . tae mean phochniyodthan te?
Are you good with chopsticks? - tae anak la cheamuoy changkuah te?
Are you good with chopsticks? - tae anak la cheamuoy changkuah te?
I had too much coffee - khnhom mean kahve chraenpek
I had too much coffee - khnhom mean kahve chraenpek
This beef is very delicious - sachko nih chhnganh nasa
This beef is very delicious - sachko nih chhnganh nasa
This restaurant has all kinds of foods. - phochniyodthan nih mean ahar krob braphet .
This restaurant has all kinds of foods. - phochniyodthan nih mean ahar krob braphet .
We do use chopsticks. - yeung brae changkuah .
We do use chopsticks. - yeung brae changkuah .
We also use a fork and spoon. - yeung ka brae sam ning slabaprea phng der .
We also use a fork and spoon. - yeung ka brae sam ning slabaprea phng der .

Travel

Airplane - y nd haoh
Airplane - y nd haoh
Airport - akasayean dthan

Airport - akasayean dthan
Bus - rth y nd krong
Bus - rth y nd krong
Bus station - chamnt lanokrong
Bus station - chamnt lanokrong
Car - rth y nd
Car - rth y nd
Flight - y nd haoh
Flight - y nd haoh
Motorbike - moto
Motorbike - moto
Bike - Kang
Bike - Kang
For business - samreab kar thveu peanechchokamm
For business - samreab kar thveu peanechchokamm
For pleasure - samreab karokamsaeant sabbay
For pleasure - samreab karokamsaeant sabbay
Hotel - sa ntha kear
Hotel - sa ntha kear
Luggage - eivean
Luggage - eivean
Parking - chamnt rth y nd
Parking - chamnt rth y nd
Passport - likhetachhlangden
Passport - likhetachhlangden
Reservation - kar kk touk
Reservation - kar kk touk
Taxi - taksai
Taxi - taksai
Ticket - saambotr
Ticket - saambotr
Tourism - tesachar
Tourism - tesachar
Train - rtihphleung(neam)
Train - rtihphleung(neam)
Train station - sthaniy rothaphleung
Train station - sthaniy rothaphleung
To travel - kar thveudamnaer
To travel - kar thveudamnaer
Help Desk - to ptrmean
Help Desk - to ptrmean
Hotel - Oat-el
Hotel - Oat-el

Guesthouse - P'dia som-nak
Guesthouse - P'dia som-nak
Room - Baan-dtoop
Room - Baan-dtoop
Single room - Baan-dtoop moy kreh-moy
Single room - Baan-dtoop moy kreh-moy
Double room - Baan-dtoop moy kreh-pee
Double room - Baan-dtoop moy kreh-pee
Embassy - Sthantout
Embassy - Sthantout
Airline - akasachar
Airline - akasachar
Cruise - chiahtouk kamsaean
Cruise - chiahtouk kamsaean
Luggage - vea li
Luggage - vea li
Tour guide - m kkou tesa tesachar
Tour guide - m kkou tesa tesachar
Immigration - antobravesa
Immigration - antobravesa
Arrivals - kar mokadl
Arrivals - kar mokadl
Suitcase - vea li
Suitcase - vea li
Navigation - neaveachar
Navigation - neaveachar
Terminal - sthaniy
Terminal - sthaniy
Passenger - anakdamnaer
Passenger - anakdamnaer
Departures - kar chakchenh
Departures - kar chakchenh
Could I see the room? - K'nyom soam merl baan-dtoop baan tay?
Could I see the room? - K'nyom soam merl baan-dtoop baan tay?
How much is the room per night? - Moy yuhp t'lay bpon-maan?
How much is the room per night? - Moy yuhp t'lay bpon-maan?
Do you accept credit cards? - tae anak ttuol yk bnnintean der ryyte?
Do you accept credit cards? - tae anak ttuol yk bnnintean der ryyte?
I have a reservation - khnhom ban thveukear kk ruochhaey
I have a reservation - khnhom ban thveukear kk ruochhaey
I'm here on business/ on vacation. - khnhom mk tinih daembi thveuchomnuonh / vissamkeal .

I'm here on business/ on vacation. - khnhom mk tinih daembi thveuchomnuonh / vissamkeal .
How much will it cost? - tae vea thlai bonman?
How much will it cost? - tae vea thlai bonman?
I want a pillow. - khnhom chngban khnaey muoy .
I want a pillow. - khnhom chngban khnaey muoy .
I want another pillow. - khnhom chngban khnaey muoytiet .
I want another pillow. - khnhom chngban khnaey muoytiet .
I want a bigger room. - khnhom chngban bantob thomcheang .
I want a bigger room. - khnhom chngban bantob thomcheang .
Please wake me up at eight o clock - saum dasa khnhom aoy phnheak now maong 8
Please wake me up at eight o clock - saum dasa khnhom aoy phnheak now maong 8
<u>Please change the sheets.</u> - saum phlasa btau r sanluk
<u>Please change the sheets.</u> - saum phlasa btau r sanluk
The fan does not work. - kanghear min damnaerkar te .
The fan does not work. - kanghear min damnaerkar te .
Can you fix it? - tae anak ach chuosachoul vea ban te?
Can you fix it? - tae anak ach chuosachoul vea ban te?
Do you have much luggage? - tae anak mean ivean chraen te?
Do you have much luggage? - tae anak mean ivean chraen te?
I want my room key. - khnhom chngban kaunsao bantob robsakhnhom
I want my room key. - khnhom chngban kaunsao bantob robsakhnhom
I'd like to rent a car - khnhom chng chuol rth y nd
I'd like to rent a car - khnhom chng chuol rth y nd
Is this seat taken? - tae kawei nih mean ke angkouy haey ryy now?
Is this seat taken? - tae kawei nih mean ke angkouy haey ryy now?
Do you know_____hotel? - Bong skol_____pojo nitan?
Do you know_____hotel? - Bong skol_____pojo nitan?
No. I don't know it. - Ot tay. Knyom ot skol.
No. I don't know it. - Ot tay. Knyom ot skol.
No problem. I know. Close to the palace. - Ot bun-yah-ha. Knyom skol. Pojo nitan chet noh veang.
No problem. I know. Close to the palace. - Ot bun-yah-ha. Knyom skol. Pojo nitan chet noh veang.
No. Go straight. Please slow down a little bit. There. - Ot tey. Doe trong. Yute yute tik. Deenouth.
No. Go straight. Please slow down a little bit. There. - Ot tey. Doe trong. Yute yute tik. Deenouth.
How long does it take to your house? - Bprau bpeel os bon-maan tov ptaeh nek?
How long does it take to your house? - Bprau bpeel os bon-maan tov ptaeh nek?
I am on the way, I went the wrong way at first. - Knom nov dtaam-plov, knom tov kos plov lauk dom boong.

I am on the way, I went the wrong way at first. - Knom nov dtaam-plov, knom tov kos plov lauk dom boong.
It is okay because I am not lost now. - Min-ey-dtee bpii-bros ey-lov nih knom min vwoong-vweeng plov dtee .
It is okay because I am not lost now. - Min-ey-dtee bpii-bros ey-lov nih knom min vwoong-vweeng plov dtee .
I don't understand - khnhom min yl te
I don't understand - khnhom min yl te
I don't speak Khmer. - khnhom min niyeay pheasaeakhmer te .
I don't speak Khmer. - khnhom min niyeay pheasaeakhmer te .
I don't speak Khmer very well. - khnhom min chehniyeay pheasaeakhmer te.
I don't speak Khmer very well. - khnhom min chehniyeay pheasaeakhmer te.
Do you speak English? - tae anak niyeay pheasaeaangklesa te?
Do you speak English? - tae anak niyeay pheasaeaangklesa te?
Does anyone here speak English? - tae mean norna mneak now tinih niyeay pheasaeaangklesa te?
Does anyone here speak English? - tae mean norna mneak now tinih niyeay pheasaeaangklesa te?
I always get nervous when I speak Khmer. - khnhom tengte phy pel khnhom niyeay pheasaeakhmer .
I always get nervous when I speak Khmer. - khnhom tengte phy pel khnhom niyeay pheasaeakhmer .
I understand you very well. - khnhom yl pi anak chbasa .
I understand you very well. - khnhom yl pi anak chbasa .
Speak slowly, please. - saum niyeay yut .
Speak slowly, please. - saum niyeay yut .
Repeat, please. - saum thveu mtong tiet .
Repeat, please. - saum thveu mtong tiet .
What does that mean? - meannytha mech?
What does that mean? - meannytha mech?
Please write that down for me - saum sarser vea samreab khnhom
Please write that down for me - saum sarser vea samreab khnhom
Could you say that again please? - anak ach niyeay mtong tiet ban te?
Could you say that again please? - anak ach niyeay mtong tiet ban te?
I don't know - khnhom mindoeng te
I don't know - khnhom mindoeng te
I'm sorry - khnhom somtos
I'm sorry - khnhom somtos
Call the flight attendant, please. - saum toursapt tow anakbamreu karhaohhaer .
Call the flight attendant, please. - saum toursapt tow anakbamreu karhaohhaer .
Can I get on the internet? - tae khnhom ach brae ainthunet ban te?
Can I get on the internet? - tae khnhom ach brae ainthunet ban te?
Can I use your phone? - tae khnhom ach brae toursapt robsa anak ban te?

Can I use your phone? - tae khnhom ach brae toursapt robsa anak ban te?
Can you show me on the map? - tae anak ach bangheanh khnhom now leu phenti ban te?
Can you show me on the map? - tae anak ach bangheanh khnhom now leu phenti ban te?
How much do I owe you? - tae khnhom chompeak anak bonman?
How much do I owe you? - tae khnhom chompeak anak bonman?
What is today's date? - tae kalobrichchhet thngainih chea avei?
What is today's date? - tae kalobrichchhet thngainih chea avei?
Where can I find public restrooms? - tae khnhom ach rk bantobtuk satharn now tinea?
Where can I find public restrooms? - tae khnhom ach rk bantobtuk satharn now tinea?
Hi, I'm trying to find my Airbnb. - suostei khnhom kampoung pyeayeam rk Airbnb robsakhnhom .
Hi, I'm trying to find my Airbnb. - suostei khnhom kampoung pyeayeam rk Airbnb robsakhnhom .
Excuse me, where did you buy that ice cream? - saumoaphytosa tae anak tinh karem noh nowenea?
Excuse me, where did you buy that ice cream? - saumoaphytosa tae anak tinh karem noh nowenea?
What is the WiFi password? - tae peakyasamngeat vea y hva y kuchea avei?
What is the WiFi password? - tae peakyasamngeat vea y hva y kuchea avei?
I lost my key. - khnhom ban batbng kaunsao r robsakhnhom .
I lost my key. - khnhom ban batbng kaunsao r robsakhnhom .
Can we pay by credit card? - tae yeung ach touteat daoy kat intean ban te?
Can we pay by credit card? - tae yeung ach touteat daoy kat intean ban te?
How does the washer work? - tae anak leangchan thveukear yeang dauchamtech?
How does the washer work? - tae anak leangchan thveukear yeang dauchamtech?
Is there an iron? - tae mean cheate dek te?
Is there an iron? - tae mean cheate dek te?
We only accept cash. - yeung ttuol yk te sachbrak bonnaoh .
We only accept cash. - yeung ttuol yk te sachbrak bonnaoh .
Do you have any vacancies? - tae anak mean kanleng tomner te?
Do you have any vacancies? - tae anak mean kanleng tomner te?
How much is it per night? - tae vea mean tamlei bonman knong muoy yb?
How much is it per night? - tae vea mean tamlei bonman knong muoy yb?
Do you need our passports? - tae anak trauvkar likhetachhlangden robsa yeung te?
Do you need our passports? - tae anak trauvkar likhetachhlangden robsa yeung te?
I'd like some toilet paper? - khnhom chngban kradeasabangkon te?
I'd like some toilet paper? - khnhom chngban kradeasabangkon te?
I am sorry, we have no more rooms available - khnhom somtosa yeung min mean bantob tiet te
I am sorry, we have no more rooms available - khnhom somtosa yeung min mean bantob tiet te

I would like to pay now - khnhom chng bngbrak ilauvnih
I would like to pay now - khnhom chng bngbrak ilauvnih
Can we go to Angkor Wat temple? - tae yeung ach tow brasaeatoangkorovott ban te?
Can we go to Angkor Wat temple? - tae yeung ach tow brasaeatoangkorovott ban te?
Is Siem Reap far from here? - tae siemrab now chhngay pi tinih te?
Is Siem Reap far from here? - tae siemrab now chhngay pi tinih te?
How do we get to Phnom Penh? - tae yeung towdl phnompenh daoy rbiebnea
How do we get to Phnom Penh? - tae yeung towdl phnompenh daoy rbiebnea
Where is the closest temple? - tae brasaeat del now chit bamphot nowenea?
Where is the closest temple? - tae brasaeat del now chit bamphot nowenea?
Which island should we go to? - tae kaoh muoy na del yeung kuor tow?
Which island should we go to? - tae kaoh muoy na del yeung kuor tow?

Day at the beach
Watch the sunset - meul thngailich
Watch the sunset - meul thngailich
Where is the beach? - tae chhner nowenea?
Where is the beach? - tae chhner nowenea?
Towel - kansaeng
Towel - kansaeng
Beach - chhner
Beach - chhner
Sand - khsaach
Sand - khsaach
Ocean - mhasamout
Ocean - mhasamout
let's go swimming - taoh tow heltuk
let's go swimming - taoh tow heltuk
Build a sandcastle - sangosang khsaach
Build a sandcastle - sangosang khsaach
Spend time with friends - chamnaypel chea muo yom mitt phokte
Spend time with friends - chamnaypel chea muo yom mitt phokte
I love the beach - khnhom sraleanh chhner
I love the beach - khnhom sraleanh chhner
what are the best beaches? - tae chhnerosamoutr la bamphot aveikhleah?
what are the best beaches? - tae chhnerosamoutr la bamphot aveikhleah?
Can you tell me the best beach in Cambodia? - tae anak ach brab khnhom chhner la bamphot now kampouchea ban te?
Can you tell me the best beach in Cambodia? - tae anak ach brab khnhom chhner la bamphot now kampouchea ban te?

Emergencies

Headache - chhukbeal
Headache - chhukbeal
Stomach ache - chhupoh
Stomach ache - chhupoh
Medicines - au sath
Medicines - au sath
Pharmacy - au sa th sthan
Pharmacy - au sa th sthan
Doctor - vechchobandet
Doctor - vechchobandet
Ambulance - lanpety
Ambulance - lanpety
Hospital - montirpety
Hospital - montirpety
Help me - chuoy khnhom phng
Help me - chuoy khnhom phng
Poison - thnapoul
Poison - thnapoul
Accident - krohthnak
Accident - krohthnak
Police - bau lisa
Police - bau lisa
Danger - krohthnak
Danger - krohthnak
Stroke - dach sarsai khuorokbal
Stroke - dach sarsai khuorokbal
Heart attack - keangbehdaung
Heart attack - keangbehdaung
Asthma - chomngu heut
Asthma - chomngu heut
Allergy - a le r hsai
Allergy - a le r hsai
Appendicitis - chomngu rleak khnengpohvien
Appendicitis - chomngu rleak khnengpohvien
Antiseptic - thnam saam leab merok
Antiseptic - thnam saam leab merok
Malaria   - chomngukrounchanh
Malaria   - chomngukrounchanh
Abortion - kar romlout kaun
Abortion - kar romlout kaun
Hallucination - kar chokpoh
Hallucination - kar chokpoh
Cancer - mharik

Cancer - mharik
Surgery - karveahkat
Surgery - karveahkat
Pain - chhucheab
Pain - chhucheab
Epidemic - kar reatatbat
Epidemic - kar reatatbat
Poisoning - kar poul
Poisoning - kar poul
Migraine - chomngu chhukbeal brakeang
Migraine - chomngu chhukbeal brakeang
Pandemic - kar reatatbat sakal
Pandemic - kar reatatbat sakal
Kidney stones - kruosa knong tam rng nom
Kidney stones - kruosa knong tam rng nom

Call the police! - saum haw bau li sa!
Call the police! - saum haw bau li sa!
Call a doctor! - saum haw vechchobandet!
Call a doctor! - saum haw vechchobandet!
Call the ambulance! - saum haw lan pety!
Call the ambulance! - saum haw lan pety!
I feel sick - khnhom mean arommo tha chhu
I feel sick - khnhom mean arommo tha chhu
Where is the closest pharmacy? - tae kanleng lk thnapety chit cheang ke now tinea?
Where is the closest pharmacy? - tae kanleng lk thnapety chit cheang ke now tinea?
It hurts here - vea chhu nowtrang nih
It hurts here - vea chhu nowtrang nih
Are you okay? - tae anak min ei te ryy?
Are you okay? - tae anak min ei te ryy?
It's urgent! - vea chea rueng bantean!
It's urgent! - vea chea rueng bantean!
Calm down! - saum trachakchett!
Calm down! - saum trachakchett!
Stop! - chhb!
Stop! - chhb!
Fire! - banh!
Fire! - banh!
Thief! - chaor!
Thief! - chaor!
Where is a good dentist? - tae petyothmenh la nowenea?
Where is a good dentist? - tae petyothmenh la nowenea?
I am constipated. - khnhom tlleamk .
I am constipated. - khnhom tlleamk .

I have a sprained ankle. - khnhom mean rbuosa k cheung .
I have a sprained ankle. - khnhom mean rbuosa k cheung .
You will have to go to the hospital. - anak nung trauv tow montirpety .
You will have to go to the hospital. - anak nung trauv tow montirpety .
I have indigestion. - khnhom mean karromleayahear .
I have indigestion. - khnhom mean karromleayahear .
I am diabetic. - khnhom mean chomngu tuknomophaem .
I am diabetic. - khnhom mean chomngu tuknomophaem .
I am allergic to penicillin. - khnhom mean a le sai tow nung b ni so ei li n .
I am allergic to penicillin. - khnhom mean a le sai tow nung b ni so ei li n .
I am pregnant. - khnhom meanophtaipoh .
I am pregnant. - khnhom meanophtaipoh .
I do not have a prescription - khnhom min mean vechchobanhchea te
I do not have a prescription - khnhom min mean vechchobanhchea te
Is it serious? - tae vea thngonthngor te?
Is it serious? - tae vea thngonthngor te?
I'm on antibiotics. - khnhom now leu thnam ang ti bi yo tich .
I'm on antibiotics. - khnhom now leu thnam ang ti bi yo tich .
I feel alright now - khnhom mean arommo tha ilauvnih
I feel alright now - khnhom mean arommo tha ilauvnih
Here is my prescription - nih chea vechchobanhchea robsakhnhom
Here is my prescription - nih chea vechchobanhchea robsakhnhom
I want to talk to a lawyer - khnhom chng niyeay cheamuoy metheavi
I want to talk to a lawyer - khnhom chng niyeay cheamuoy metheavi
I want to talk to the American embassy. - khnhom chng niyeay cheamuoy sthantout amerik .
I want to talk to the American embassy. - khnhom chng niyeay cheamuoy sthantout amerik .

Getting around

Excuse me! (to ask someone) - somtosa!(daembi suor anaknea mneak)
Excuse me! (to ask someone) - somtosa!(daembi suor anaknea mneak)
Can you show me? - tae anak ach bangheanh phlauv khnhom ban te?
Can you show me? - tae anak ach bangheanh phlauv khnhom ban te?
I'm lost - khnhom vongvengophlauv
I'm lost - khnhom vongvengophlauv
I'm not from here - khnhom minmen chea anak rsanow tinih te
I'm not from here - khnhom minmen chea anak rsanow tinih te
Can I help you? - tae khnhom ach chuoy anak ban te?
Can I help you? - tae khnhom ach chuoy anak ban te?
Can you help me? - tae anak ach chuoy khnhom ban te?
Can you help me? - tae anak ach chuoy khnhom ban te?

It's near here - vea now chit nih
It's near here - vea now chit nih
It's far from here - vea now chhngay piti nih
It's far from here - vea now chhngay piti nih
Go straight - daertow aoy trang
Go straight - daertow aoy trang
Turn left - btchhveng
Turn left - btchhveng
Turn right - btsdam
Turn right - btsdam
One moment please! - saum rngcham muoyophlet!
One moment please! - saum rngcham muoyophlet!
Come with me! - daertam khnhom mk!
Come with me! - daertam khnhom mk!
How can I get to the museum? - tae khnhom ach towkean sar m nti daoy rbiebnea?
How can I get to the museum? - tae khnhom ach towkean sar m nti daoy rbiebnea?
How long does it take to get there? - tae towkean tinoh trauv chamnaypel bonman?
How long does it take to get there? - tae towkean tinoh trauv chamnaypel bonman?
Downtown - tikrong
Downtown - tikrong
Near - chit
Near - chit
Far - chhngay
Far - chhngay
Right - sdam
Right - sdam
Left - chhveng
Left - chhveng
in front of - kang mohk
in front of - kang mohk
Behind - kang krao·y
Behind - kang krao·y
Straight - trang
Straight - trang
There - tinoh
There - tinoh
Here - tinih
Here - tinih
To walk - daer
To walk - daer
To drive - baekabr
To drive - baekabr
To turn - bt

To turn - bt
Traffic light - phleung chreachr
Traffic light - phleung chreachr
where, which - naa
where, which - naa
Where are you going? - lohk, ayn·chern ðeuw naa?
Where are you going? - lohk, ayn·chern ðeuw naa?
Where is the school? - sah·laa neuw ei naa
Where is the school? - sah·laa neuw ei naa
Where is the guesthouse? - puh·ðay·uh suhm·nahk neuw ei naa?
Where is the guesthouse? - puh·ðay·uh suhm·nahk neuw ei naa?
That's right! - maen hao·y
That's right! - maen hao·y
That's not right. - muhn maen ðay
That's not right. - muhn maen ðay

What would you like? - lohk ðrow-gaa ei
What would you like? - lohk ðrow-gaa ei
I want some cigarettes. - kuh·nyohm ðrow-gaa baa·rei
I want some cigarettes. - kuh·nyohm ðrow-gaa baa·rei
Do you want some matches? - lohk jawng baan cher·gooh ðay
Do you want some matches? - lohk jawng baan cher·gooh ðay
Here are the cigarettes and matches. - nih baa·rei nuhng cher·gooh
Here are the cigarettes and matches. - nih baa·rei nuhng cher·gooh
What time does the last train come? - tae rothaphleung chongokraoy mokadl maong bonman?
What time does the last train come? - tae rothaphleung chongokraoy mokadl maong bonman?
The train is late. - rothaphleung yut .
The train is late. - rothaphleung yut .
How long does the trip take? - tae kar thveudamnaer chamnaypel bonman?
How long does the trip take? - tae kar thveudamnaer chamnaypel bonman?
What is the next stop? - tae chamnt banteab kuchea avei?
What is the next stop? - tae chamnt banteab kuchea avei?
I would like to rent a car. - khnhom chng chuol lan .
I would like to rent a car. - khnhom chng chuol lan .
I have to cancel my reservation. - khnhom trauvte loubchaol kar kk robsakhnhom .
I have to cancel my reservation. - khnhom trauvte loubchaol kar kk robsakhnhom .
How do I get to the airport? - tae khnhom trauv tow akasayean dthan yeang dauchamtech?

How do I get to the airport? - tae khnhom trauv tow akasayean dthan yeang dauchamtech?
What platform is my train leaving from? - tae rothaphleung robsakhnhom chakchenh pi na?
What platform is my train leaving from? - tae rothaphleung robsakhnhom chakchenh pi na?
I'm in a hurry! - khnhom branhab!
I'm in a hurry! - khnhom branhab!
How much do I owe you? - tae khnhom chompeak anak bonman?
How much do I owe you? - tae khnhom chompeak anak bonman?
Do you accept dollars? - tae anak prom ttuol louy dollar te?
Do you accept dollars? - tae anak prom ttuol louy dollar te?
Do you accept British pounds? - tae anak ttuol yk phaon angklesa te?
Do you accept British pounds? - tae anak ttuol yk phaon angklesa te?
Can you change money for me? - tae anak ach btau r brak samreab khnhom ban te?
Can you change money for me? - tae anak ach btau r brak samreab khnhom ban te?
Where can I get money changed? - tae khnhom ach roklouy ban nowenea?
Where can I get money changed? - tae khnhom ach roklouy ban nowenea?
What is the exchange rate? - tae atra btau r brak kuchea avei?
What is the exchange rate? - tae atra btau r brak kuchea avei?
Is there commission? - tae mean knkammokear te?
Is there commission? - tae mean knkammokear te?
What is today's date? - tae kalobrichchhet thngainih chea avei?
What is today's date? - tae kalobrichchhet thngainih chea avei?
Where is an automatic teller machine (ATM)? - tae measain dakabrak svyobravotte (e thi oe m) nowenea?
Where is an automatic teller machine (ATM)? - tae measain dakabrak svyobravotte (e thi oe m) nowenea?
Where is the restaurant? - pow·chuh·nee·yuh·taan neuw ei naa?
Where is the restaurant? - pow·chuh·nee·yuh·taan neuw ei naa?

Talking about the Weather
Cloudy - mean popk
Cloudy - mean popk
Cold - trachak
Cold - trachak
Foggy - chohapt

Foggy - chohapt
Humid - saamnaem
Humid - saamnaem
Hot - ktaw
Hot - ktaw
Warm - kdaw unh
Warm - kdaw unh
Rain - phlieng
Rain - phlieng
Rainy - del mean phlieng thleak
Rainy - del mean phlieng thleak
Snow - pril
Snow - pril
Snowing - kar thleakpril
Snowing - kar thleakpril
Sun - thngai
Sun - thngai
Sunny - mean ponluthngai
Sunny - mean ponluthngai
Wind - khyal
Wind - khyal
Windy - khsa l khlang
Windy - khsa l khlang
Spring - niteakhordauv
Spring - niteakhordauv
Summer - kimhordauv
Summer - kimhordauv
Autumn - sarotordauv
Autumn - sarotordauv
Winter - seserordauv
Winter - seserordauv
Umbrella - chhtr
Umbrella - chhtr
Storm - pyouh
Storm - pyouh
Rainbow - i nth nou

Rainbow - i nth nou

Climate - akasatheato

Climate - akasatheato

Landslide - kar rel bak dei

Landslide - kar rel bak dei

Eruption - kar phtoh
Eruption - kar phtoh
Earthquake - karoronhchuoydei
Earthquake - karoronhchuoydei
Fire - phleung
Fire - phleung
Tsunami - saou na mi
Tsunami - saou na mi
Thunder - phkarlan
Thunder - phkarlan
Lightning - ronteah
Lightning - ronteah
Drought - kroh reangosnguot
Drought - kroh reangosnguot
Blizzard - pyouh pril
Blizzard - pyouh pril
Today is nice weather - thngainih akasatheato la
Today is nice weather - thngainih akasatheato la
Yesterday was bad weather - msailminh akasatheato minola
Yesterday was bad weather - msailminh akasatheato minola
It is raining - mekh phlieng
It is raining - mekh phlieng
It is sunny - mekhbaekathngai
It is sunny - mekhbaekathngai
It is windy - mekh thleak khyal
It is windy - mekh thleak khyal
It is cold - mekh trachak
It is cold - mekh trachak

Languages and Countries

English - angklesa
English - angklesa
Arabic - areab
Arabic - areab
Chinese - chen
Chinese - chen

Brazilian - bresail
Brazilian - bresail
French - barang
French - barang
German - a llu mng
German - a llu mng
Greek - krek
Greek - krek
Hebrew - he brau
Hebrew - he brau
Hindi - hendau
Hindi - hendau
Irish - ierolng
Irish - ierolng
Italian - aiteali
Italian - aiteali
Japanese - chbon
Japanese - chbon
Korean - kaure
Korean - kaure
Portuguese - prtouyohkal
Portuguese - prtouyohkal
Russian - roussai
Russian - roussai
Spanish - esbanh
Spanish - esbanh
Swedish - saou y ed
Swedish - saou y ed
I speak Italian - khnhom niyeay pheasaea aiteali
I speak Italian - khnhom niyeay pheasaea aiteali
I want to learn Spanish - khnhom chng rien pheasaea esbanh
I want to learn Spanish - khnhom chng rien pheasaea esbanh
My mother tongue is German - pheasaea daem robsakhnhom ku allumng
My mother tongue is German - pheasaea daem robsakhnhom ku allumng
I love the Japanese language - khnhom chaulchett pheasaea chbon
I love the Japanese language - khnhom chaulchett pheasaea chbon
I don't speak Korean - khnhom min niyeay pheasaea kaure te
I don't speak Korean - khnhom min niyeay pheasaea kaure te
Spanish is easy to learn - esbanh chea pheasaea sruol rien
Spanish is easy to learn - esbanh chea pheasaea sruol rien
British - angklesa
British - angklesa
American - amerik

American - amerik
Israeli - aisreael
Israeli - aisreael
Japanese - chbon
Japanese - chbon
Moroccan - mearok
Moroccan - mearok
Indian - inda
Indian - inda
I'm Italian - khnhom chea choncheate aiteali
I'm Italian - khnhom chea choncheate aiteali
My father is Greek - au pouk robsakhnhom chea choncheate krech
My father is Greek - au pouk robsakhnhom chea choncheate krech
I love French cheese - khnhom chett brahok brau mea barang
I love French cheese - khnhom chett brahok brau mea barang
My wife is Korean - braponth robsakhnhom chea choncheate kaure
My wife is Korean - braponth robsakhnhom chea choncheate kaure
I have an American car - khnhom mean lan phlit now amerik
I have an American car - khnhom mean lan phlit now amerik
He has a Moroccan rug - khnhom mean prom phlit now mearok
He has a Moroccan rug - khnhom mean prom phlit now mearok
Britain - angklesa
Britain - angklesa
China - chen
China - chen
Ireland - ierolng
Ireland - ierolng
Greece - krech
Greece - krech
Italy - aiteali
Italy - aiteali
I live in America - khnhom rsanow bratesa amerik
I live in America - khnhom rsanow bratesa amerik
I came from Spain - khnhom mk pi bratesa allumng
I came from Spain - khnhom mk pi bratesa allumng
Japan is a beautiful country - chbon chea bratesa da srasa saat
Japan is a beautiful country - chbon chea bratesa da srasa saat
I want to go to Germany - khnhom chng tow bratesa allumng
I want to go to Germany - khnhom chng tow bratesa allumng
I was born in Italy - khnhom kaet now bratesa aiteali
I was born in Italy - khnhom kaet now bratesa aiteali
Have you ever been to India? - tae anak thleab tow bratesa inda te?
Have you ever been to India? - tae anak thleab tow bratesa inda te?

At School

Book - sievphow
Book - sievphow
Library - bannaly
Library - bannaly
Chair - kawei
Chair - kawei
Notebook - sievphowsarser
Notebook - sievphowsarser
School - salarien
School - salarien
To speak - sdab
To speak - sdab
Books - sievphow cheachraen
Books - sievphow cheachraen
Desk - tosarser
Desk - tosarser
Paper - kradeasa
Paper - kradeasa
Laptop - le bathb
Laptop - le bathb
University - mhavityealy
University - mhavityealy
To listen - niyeay
To listen - niyeay
Pen - bich ser ser
Pen - bich ser ser
Student - sessa / ni se tsa
Student - sessa / ni se tsa
Page - tompr
Page - tompr
Question - saamnuor
Question - saamnuor
To write - sarser
To write - sarser
To think - kit
To think - kit
Dictionary - vochneanoukram
Dictionary - vochneanoukram
Teacher - krou
Teacher - krou
Pencil - khmawdai
Pencil - khmawdai

Answer - chamleuy
Answer - chamleuy
To read - an
To read - an
To understand - yl
To understand - yl
Chalk - dei·saw
Chalk - dei·saw
Blackboard - kuh·dar-key·an
Blackboard - kuh·dar-key·an
Library - bannaly
Library - bannaly
Notebook - sievphow kttra
Notebook - sievphow kttra
Glue - ka v
Glue - ka v
Scissors - kantrai
Scissors - kantrai
Eraser - ch·ar-loub
Eraser - ch·ar-loub
Table - đohk
Table - đohk
Sentence - klee·ah
Sentence - klee·ah
That's called a pencil. - ruh·bawh nooh gay haa·ew taa k·mao-đai
That's called a pencil. - ruh·bawh nooh gay haa·ew taa k·mao-đai
How is that word pronounced? - pe·ak nooh merl taa mait
How is that word pronounced? - pe·ak nooh merl taa mait
That word is pronounced "gao·ei". - pe·ak nooh merl taa gao·ei
That word is pronounced "gao·ei". - pe·ak nooh merl taa gao·ei
Please read that sentence. - sohm merl klee·ah nooh
Please read that sentence. - sohm merl klee·ah nooh
Excuse me, which sentence? - sohm-đoh, klee·ah naa?
Excuse me, which sentence? - sohm-đoh, klee·ah naa?
The same sentence? - klee·ah đoe·dahl
The same sentence? - klee·ah đoe·dahl
No, the next sentence. - muhn maen đay, klee·ah bawn·đo·uhp
No, the next sentence. - muhn maen đay, klee·ah bawn·đo·uhp
How is that sentence translated? - klee·ah nooh ƀrai taa mait
How is that sentence translated? - klee·ah nooh ƀrai taa mait
Please answer my question(s) - sohm ch·laey saam·noo·er kuh·nyom
Please answer my question(s) - sohm ch·laey saam·noo·er kuh·nyom

why, how is it that? - mait-gaa
why, how is it that? - mait-gaa
Why can't you answer - mait-gaa ch·laey muhn baan
Why can't you answer - mait-gaa ch·laey muhn baan
I didn't understand some of the words. - pe·ak klah kuh·nyom muhn yuhl đay
I didn't understand some of the words. - pe·ak klah kuh·nyom muhn yuhl đay
Please make a sentence with this word. - jow twer klee·ah nung pe·ak nih
Please make a sentence with this word. - jow twer klee·ah nung pe·ak nih
I have a question - khnhom mean saamnuor
I have a question - khnhom mean saamnuor
What's the name of that book? - tae sievphow noh chhmoh avei?
What's the name of that book? - tae sievphow noh chhmoh avei?
Do you have a book? - lohk, mee·uhn see·iw-peuw đay
Do you have a book? - lohk, mee·uhn see·iw-peuw đay
Please open your books. - sohm lohk baok see·iw-peuw
Please open your books. - sohm lohk baok see·iw-peuw
What page (should we open to)? - baok đom·ƀu·or tii-ƀohn·maan
What page (should we open to)? - baok đom·ƀu·or tii-ƀohn·maan
Please close your books - sohm buht see·iw-peuw
Please close your books - sohm buht see·iw-peuw
Please say after me. - sohm taa đam kuh·nyom
Please say after me. - sohm taa đam kuh·nyom
all together - đay·uhng-awh knea
all together - đay·uhng-awh knea
That is a book - nooh goo jee·aa see·iw-peuw
That is a book - nooh goo jee·aa see·iw-peuw
What subject is your best? - tae moukhvichcha avei del la bamphot?
What subject is your best? - tae moukhvichcha avei del la bamphot?
What subject do you most like? - moukhvichcha na del anak chaulchett cheangke?
What subject do you most like? - moukhvichcha na del anak chaulchett cheangke?
I am good at Chemistry. - khnhom pouke khang kimivityea .
I am good at Chemistry. - khnhom pouke khang kimivityea .
I am very bad at math - khnhom pouke knetvitya nasa
I am very bad at math - khnhom pouke knetvitya nasa
My favorite subject in school is math - moukhvichcha del khnhom chaulchett cheangke now sala ku knetvitya
My favorite subject in school is math - moukhvichcha del khnhom chaulchett cheangke now sala ku knetvitya
Answer the math problem. - chhlaey banhhea knetvitya .
Answer the math problem. - chhlaey banhhea knetvitya .
What page? - tae tompr avei?
What page? - tae tompr avei?

How do you spell...? - tae anak brakb dauchamtech ... ?
How do you spell...? - tae anak brakb dauchamtech ... ?

Around the house

Bed - kre
Bed - kre
Bedroom - bantobdek
Bedroom - bantobdek
Carpet - kamrealoprom
Carpet - kamrealoprom
Ceiling - pi dan
Ceiling - pi dan
Chair - kawei
Chair - kawei
Computer - kompyoutr
Computer - kompyoutr
Desk - tosarser
Desk - tosarser
Door - tvear
Door - tvear
Furniture - krueng sanghea rum
Furniture - krueng sanghea rum
House - phteah
House - phteah
Kitchen - phteahbay
Kitchen - phteahbay
Refrigerator - toutukakk
Refrigerator - toutukakk
Roof - dambaul
Roof - dambaul
Room - bantob
Room - bantob
Table - to
Table - to
Television - tourotossaa
Television - tourotossaa
Toilet - bangkon
Toilet - bangkon
Window - bangauoch
Window - bangauoch
Stove - changkran
Stove - changkran

Wall - chonhcheang
Wall - chonhcheang
Cupboard - tou dak chan
Cupboard - tou dak chan
Bench - leng chea keilakr bamroung
Bench - leng chea keilakr bamroung
Bathtub - angngouttuk
Bathtub - angngouttuk
Mattress - pouk
Mattress - pouk
Shower - phkachhouk
Shower - phkachhouk
Sink - lich
Sink - lich
Pillowcase - khnaey
Pillowcase - khnaey
Drawer - that
Drawer - that
Rug - prom
Rug - prom
Tiles - kbueng
Tiles - kbueng
Carpet - kam real prom
Carpet - kam real prom
Furniture - krueng sanghea rum
Furniture - krueng sanghea rum
Vacuum - measainbaum thouli
Vacuum - measainbaum thouli
Freezer - mea sei n toek k k
Freezer - mea sei n toek k k
Dishwasher - mea so ei n long chan
Dishwasher - mea so ei n long chan
Microwave - mikrau vev
Microwave - mikrau vev
Napkin - na bau khi n
Napkin - na bau khi n
Saucepan - tukachrolk
Saucepan - tukachrolk
I'm watching television - khnhom kampoungte meul tourotossaa
I'm watching television - khnhom kampoungte meul tourotossaa
Can you close the door? - tae anak betotvear ban te?
Can you close the door? - tae anak betotvear ban te?
This room is very big - bantob nih thom nasa

This room is very big - bantob nih thom nasa
I need to use the toilet - khnhom trauvkar brae bangkon
I need to use the toilet - khnhom trauvkar brae bangkon
Can you open the window? - tae anak ach baek bangauoch ban te?
Can you open the window? - tae anak ach baek bangauoch ban te?
I need to use the computer - khnhom trauvkar brae kompyoutr
I need to use the computer - khnhom trauvkar brae kompyoutr
We live on the first floor. - yeung rsanow chean timuoy .
We live on the first floor. - yeung rsanow chean timuoy .
The building is very old. - akear nih chasa nasa .
The building is very old. - akear nih chasa nasa .
There's no elevator - min mean karkatbanthoy te
There's no elevator - min mean karkatbanthoy te
We just moved to a new house - yeung teubte phlasa towphteah thmei
We just moved to a new house - yeung teubte phlasa towphteah thmei
Come on, let me give you a tour - saum anhcheunh mk khnhom aoy anakdamnaer tossaankechch muoy
Come on, let me give you a tour - saum anhcheunh mk khnhom aoy anakdamnaer tossaankechch muoy
This room will be my office! - bantob nih nung klaycha kariyealy robsakhnhom!
This room will be my office! - bantob nih nung klaycha kariyealy robsakhnhom!
The kitchen is my favorite room. - phteahbay kuchea bantob del khnhom chaulchett bamphot .
The kitchen is my favorite room. - phteahbay kuchea bantob del khnhom chaulchett bamphot .
Let's go to the kitchen - taoh tow phteahbay
Let's go to the kitchen - taoh tow phteahbay

Places to go

Bank - theanea kear
Bank - theanea kear
Forest - prei
Forest - prei
Lake - boeng
Lake - boeng
Moon - lokkhe / preahchnt
Moon - lokkhe / preahchnt
Hospital - montirpety
Hospital - montirpety
Garden - suonochbar
Garden - suonochbar
Sea - samoutr

Sea - samoutr
Stars - phkay
Stars - phkay
Desert - vealokhsaach
Desert - vealokhsaach
Island - kaoh
Island - kaoh
Sky - mekh
Sky - mekh
Mountain - phnom
Mountain - phnom
Earth - phendei
Earth - phendei
River - tonle
River - tonle
Sun - preahatity
Sun - preahatity
Beach - chhnerosamoutr
Beach - chhnerosamoutr
I can see the stars - khnhom ach meulkheunh phkay cheachraen
I can see the stars - khnhom ach meulkheunh phkay cheachraen
This is a beautiful garden - nih chea suonochbar da saat muoy
This is a beautiful garden - nih chea suonochbar da saat muoy
I want to go to the beach - khnhom chng tow leng chhnerokhsaach
I want to go to the beach - khnhom chng tow leng chhnerokhsaach
The moon is full tonight - yb nih preah chnt reah penhovng
The moon is full tonight - yb nih preah chnt reah penhovng
What are the provinces in Cambodia? - tae khett nakhleah nowknong bratesa kampouchea?
What are the provinces in Cambodia? - tae khett nakhleah nowknong bratesa kampouchea?
The ground is very wet. - deisaem nasa .
The ground is very wet. - deisaem nasa

Jobs

Doctor - vechchobandet
Doctor - vechchobandet
Student - sessa / ni se tsa
Student - sessa / ni se tsa
Actor - tuokon brosa
Actor - tuokon brosa
Policeman - baulisa
Policeman - baulisa

Singer - anakachamrieng
Singer - anakachamrieng
Actress - tuokon srei
Actress - tuokon srei
Teacher - kroubangrien
Teacher - kroubangrien
Engineer - visvakr
Engineer - visvakr
Nurse - ki lea nou dtha k yi ka
Nurse - ki lea nou dtha k yi ka
Businessman - peanechchokr
Businessman - peanechchokr
Artist - selbokr
Artist - selbokr
Translator - anakabakabre
Translator - anakabakabre
Factory - rongochak
Factory - rongochak
sugar refinery - rongochakr chamreanh skar
sugar refinery - rongochakr chamreanh skar
Distillery - measainbaum tuk
Distillery - measainbaum tuk
rubber factory - rongochakr kawsaou
rubber factory - rongochakr kawsaou
I'm looking for a job - khnhom kampoung svengork karngear thveu
I'm looking for a job - khnhom kampoung svengork karngear thveu
He is a policeman - keat chea baulisa
He is a policeman - keat chea baulisa
I'm a new employee - khnhom chea bokkolik thmei
I'm a new employee - khnhom chea bokkolik thmei
I'm an artist - khnhom chea vichetrakr
I'm an artist - khnhom chea vichetrakr
She is a singer - neang chea anakachamrieng
She is a singer - neang chea anakachamrieng
I have a lot of experience - khnhom meanobatpisaoth chraen chhnam
I have a lot of experience - khnhom meanobatpisaoth chraen chhnam
My work place is not far from here. - Kan-leng tver-ka ro-bos khnom nov min chngaay bpii ti-nis te.
My work place is not far from here. - Kan-leng tver-ka ro-bos khnom nov min chngaay bpii ti-nis te.

Conversation

Yes - Jah
Yes - Jah
No - Ot-dae
No - Ot-dae
let's go - Da-doh
let's go - Da-doh
Long time no see - khan chuobaknea yourhaey
Long time no see - khan chuobaknea yourhaey
I missed you - khnhom nuk anak
I missed you - khnhom nuk anak
What's new? - tae mean avei thmei?
What's new? - tae mean avei thmei?
Nothing new - kmeanoavei thmei te
Nothing new - kmeanoavei thmei te
Make yourself at home! - saum thveu khluon aoy dauch nowphteah robsa anak tow!
Make yourself at home! - saum thveu khluon aoy dauch nowphteah robsa anak tow!
Have a good trip - saum thveudamnaer daoy sovotthephap
Have a good trip - saum thveudamnaer daoy sovotthephap
Do you speak English? - tae anak chehniyeay pheasaeaangklesa der ryyte?
Do you speak English? - tae anak chehniyeay pheasaeaangklesa der ryyte?
Just a little - niyeay ban bantichabantuoch
Just a little - niyeay ban bantichabantuoch
<u>Do you speak Cambodian ?</u> - tae anak niyeay pheasaeakhmer te?
<u>Do you speak Cambodian ?</u> - tae anak niyeay pheasaeakhmer te?
I still don' t understand what you just said. - khnhom nowte min yl pi avei del anak teubte niyeay .
I still don' t understand what you just said. - khnhom nowte min yl pi avei del anak teubte niyeay .
What is this called in Cambodian ? - tae avei delke hawtha chea pheasaeakhmer?
What is this called in Cambodian ? - tae avei delke hawtha chea pheasaeakhmer?
Do you understand all of it ? - tae anak yl pi vea te?
Do you understand all of it ? - tae anak yl pi vea te?
Thank you for helping me learn more Cambodian. - saum arkoun del ban chuoy khnhom rien pheasaeakhmer banthem tiet .
Thank you for helping me learn more Cambodian. - saum arkoun del ban chuoy khnhom rien pheasaeakhmer banthem tiet .
I want to learn Cambodian. - khnhom chng rien pheasaeakhmer .
I want to learn Cambodian. - khnhom chng rien pheasaeakhmer .
I understand some of it. - khnhom yl pi vea khleah .
I understand some of it. - khnhom yl pi vea khleah .
What does this word mean? - tae peaky nih meanny yeang dauchamtech?
What does this word mean? - tae peaky nih meanny yeang dauchamtech?
It is very difficult for me. - vea pitchea lombak nasa samreab khnhom .

It is very difficult for me. - vea pitchea lombak nasa samreab khnhom.
Do you have a Cambodian-English dictionary at home ? - tae anak mean vochneanoukram khmer - angklesa nowphteah te?
Do you have a Cambodian-English dictionary at home ? - tae anak mean vochneanoukram khmer - angklesa nowphteah te?
I don't know how to say it in Cambodian. - khnhom min chehniyeay chea pheasaeakhmer te.
I don't know how to say it in Cambodian. - khnhom min chehniyeay chea pheasaeakhmer te.
I am learning more Cambodian every single day. - khnhom kampoung rien pheasaeakhmer kante chraen chea riengrealthngai.
I am learning more Cambodian every single day. - khnhom kampoung rien pheasaeakhmer kante chraen chea riengrealthngai.
Did I say it right? - tae khnhom niyeay trauv te?
Did I say it right? - tae khnhom niyeay trauv te?
Can you write Cambodian? - tae anak ach sarser pheasaeakhmer ban te?
Can you write Cambodian? - tae anak ach sarser pheasaeakhmer ban te?
It is quite easy. - vea ngeayosruol nasa.
It is quite easy. - vea ngeayosruol nasa.
We will talk to you again in a week. - yeung nung niyeay cheamuoy anak mtong tiet knong muoy sa bta.
We will talk to you again in a week. - yeung nung niyeay cheamuoy anak mtong tiet knong muoy sa bta.
It's time for me to go back to work. - dahl maong kuh·nyom đtrow·lop đeuw twer-gaa hao·y
It's time for me to go back to work. - dahl maong kuh·nyom đtrow·lop đeuw twer-gaa hao·y
I have to go to work too. - kuh·nyom gaw đrow đeuw twer-gaa dai
I have to go to work too. - kuh·nyom gaw đrow đeuw twer-gaa dai
Then [let's] walk back together - ahn·chung dai đeuw viyn jee·aa-muy-knea
Then [let's] walk back together - ahn·chung dai đeuw viyn jee·aa-muy-knea
What's your name? - tae anak chhmoh avei der?
What's your name? - tae anak chhmoh avei der?
My name is (John Doe) - khnhom chhmoh (dyan dou)
My name is (John Doe) - khnhom chhmoh (dyan dou)
Mr.../ Mrs. .../ Miss... - lok... / anakasrei...... / kanhnhea…
Mr.../ Mrs. .../ Miss... - lok... / anakasrei...... / kanhnhea…
Nice to meet you! - rikreay nasa del ban chuob anak!
Nice to meet you! - rikreay nasa del ban chuob anak!
You're very kind! - anak chettala nasa!
You're very kind! - anak chettala nasa!
Where are you from? - tae anak mk pinea?
Where are you from? - tae anak mk pinea?

I'm from the U.S - khnhom mk pi bratesa amerik
I'm from the U.S - khnhom mk pi bratesa amerik
I'm American - khnhom chea choncheate amerik
I'm American - khnhom chea choncheate amerik
Where do you live? - tae anak rsanow tinea?
Where do you live? - tae anak rsanow tinea?
I live in the U.S - khnhom rsanow bratesa amerik
I live in the U.S - khnhom rsanow bratesa amerik
Do you like it here? - tae anak chaulchett tinih te?
Do you like it here? - tae anak chaulchett tinih te?
Who? - norna?
Who? - norna?
Where? - kanlengna?
Where? - kanlengna?
How? - rbiebnea?
How? - rbiebnea?
When? - pelna?
When? - pelna?
Why? - hetoavei?
Why? - hetoavei?
What? - avei?
What? - avei?
By train - tam rothaphleung
By train - tam rothaphleung
By car - tam rth y nd
By car - tam rth y nd
By bus - tam rth y nd krong
By bus - tam rth y nd krong
By taxi - tam taksai
By taxi - tam taksai
By airplane - tam y nd haoh
By airplane - tam y nd haoh
Malta is a wonderful country - mealta kuchea bratesa da srasa saat
Malta is a wonderful country - mealta kuchea bratesa da srasa saat
What do you do for a living? - tae anak brakabmoukharobr avei der?
What do you do for a living? - tae anak brakabmoukharobr avei der?
I'm a (teacher/ artist/ engineer) - khnhom chea (kroubangrien / selbokr / visvakr)
I'm a (teacher/ artist/ engineer) - khnhom chea (kroubangrien / selbokr / visvakr)
I like Maltese - khnhom chaulchett choncheate mealta
I like Maltese - khnhom chaulchett choncheate mealta
I'm trying to learn Maltese - khnhom kampoungte pyeayeam rien pheasaea mealta
I'm trying to learn Maltese - khnhom kampoungte pyeayeam rien pheasaea mealta
Oh! That's good! - au! pitchea la!

Oh! That's good! - au! pitchea la!
Can I practice with you - tae khnhom ach anouvott cheamuoy anak ban ban te?
Can I practice with you - tae khnhom ach anouvott cheamuoy anak ban ban te?
How old are you? - tae anak ayou bonman?
How old are you? - tae anak ayou bonman?
I'm (twenty, thirty...) Years old - khnhom mean ayou (muoy mphei samseb...) chhnam
I'm (twenty, thirty...) Years old - khnhom mean ayou (muoy mphei samseb...) chhnam
Are you married? - tae anak riebkear haey ryy now?
Are you married? - tae anak riebkear haey ryy now?
Do you have children? - tae anak meankaun te?
Do you have children? - tae anak meankaun te?
I have to go - khnhom trauv tow haey
I have to go - khnhom trauv tow haey
I will be right back! - khnhom nung tralb mokvinh phleam!
I will be right back! - khnhom nung tralb mokvinh phleam!
This - nih
This - nih
That - noh
That - noh
Here - tinih
Here - tinih
There - tinoh
There - tinoh
It was nice meeting you - rikreay del ban chuob anak
It was nice meeting you - rikreay del ban chuob anak
Take this! - yk tow!(nowpel aoy robsa avei muo uo y)
Take this! - yk tow!(nowpel aoy robsa avei muo uo y)
Do you like it? - tae anak chaulchett vea te?
Do you like it? - tae anak chaulchett vea te?
I really like it! - khnhom pitchea chaulchett vea men!
I really like it! - khnhom pitchea chaulchett vea men!
I'm just kidding - khnhom kreante lengsaech te
I'm just kidding - khnhom kreante lengsaech te
He is a student. - Kat keu chea niset.
He is a student. - Kat keu chea niset.
We are police officers. - Yueng chea muntrey polis.
We are police officers. - Yueng chea muntrey polis.
She is hungry. - Neang klean.
She is hungry. - Neang klean.
I'm hungry - khnhom khlean
I'm hungry - khnhom khlean
I'm thirsty - khnhom srektuk
I'm thirsty - khnhom srektuk

He is tall. - Kat kpous.
He is tall. - Kat kpous.
Phnom Penh is big. - Phnom Penh thom.
Phnom Penh is big. - Phnom Penh thom.
We are lovers. - Yeung keu chea sraleanh.
We are lovers. - Yeung keu chea sraleanh.
They are rich. - Pouk ke sambour beb.
They are rich. - Pouk ke sambour beb.
In The Morning - nowpel pruk
In The Morning - nowpel pruk
In the evening - nowpel lngeach
In the evening - nowpel lngeach
At Night - nowpel yb
At Night - nowpel yb
Really! - pitmen!
Really! - pitmen!
Look! - meul noh!
Look! - meul noh!
Hurry up! - branhab laeng!
Hurry up! - branhab laeng!
What? - avei?
What? - avei?
Where? - kanlengna?
Where? - kanlengna?
What time is it? - tae maong bonman haey?
What time is it? - tae maong bonman haey?
It's 10 o'clock - vea maong 10 kt
It's 10 o'clock - vea maong 10 kt
Give me this! - aoy robsa nih mk khnhom!
Give me this! - aoy robsa nih mk khnhom!
I love you - khnhom sralanh anak
I love you - khnhom sralanh anak
Are you free tomorrow evening? - lngeach thngaisaek tae anak tomner te?
Are you free tomorrow evening? - lngeach thngaisaek tae anak tomner te?
I would like to invite you for dinner - khnhom chng bbuol anak tow nheabay pelolngeach!
I would like to invite you for dinner - khnhom chng bbuol anak tow nheabay pelolngeach!
Are you married? - tae anak riebkear haey ryy now?
Are you married? - tae anak riebkear haey ryy now?
I'm single - khnhom now liv
I'm single - khnhom now liv
Would you marry me? - riebkear cheamuoy khnhom ban te?
Would you marry me? - riebkear cheamuoy khnhom ban te?
Can I have your phone number? - tae khnhom ach som lekhtoursapt robsa anak ban te?

Can I have your phone number? - tae khnhom ach som lekhtoursapt robsa anak ban te?
Can I have your email? - tae khnhom ach som asayodthan ai me l robsa anak ban te?
Can I have your email? - tae khnhom ach som asayodthan ai me l robsa anak ban te?
You look beautiful! (to a woman) - anak meul tow saat nasa!(niyeay towkean mnoussa srei)
You look beautiful! (to a woman) - anak meul tow saat nasa!(niyeay towkean mnoussa srei)
You have a beautiful name - chhmoh robsa anak pi roh nasa
You have a beautiful name - chhmoh robsa anak pi roh nasa
This is my wife - nih chea braponth robsakhnhom
This is my wife - nih chea braponth robsakhnhom
This is my husband - nih chea bdei robsakhnhom
This is my husband - nih chea bdei robsakhnhom
This is my son - nih kuchea kaunobrosa robsakhnhom
This is my son - nih kuchea kaunobrosa robsakhnhom
This is my daughter - nih chea kaunosrei robsakhnhom
This is my daughter - nih chea kaunosrei robsakhnhom
I'm here with a group - khnhom now tinih cheamuoy krom
I'm here with a group - khnhom now tinih cheamuoy krom
I'm here on business - khnhom now tinih samreab achivokam
I'm here on business - khnhom now tinih samreab achivokam
I have an accent - khnhom meankar sangkot saamleng
I have an accent - khnhom meankar sangkot saamleng
What have you been up to? - tae anak ban thveuavei khleah?
What have you been up to? - tae anak ban thveuavei khleah?
Do you have any plans for the summer? - tae anak mean phenkar samreab rdauv ktaw te?
Do you have any plans for the summer? - tae anak mean phenkar samreab rdauv ktaw te?
What kind of music do you like? - tae tantrei braphet na del anak chaulchett?
What kind of music do you like? - tae tantrei braphet na del anak chaulchett?
I had a lot of fun! - khnhom meankar sabbay chraen!
I had a lot of fun! - khnhom meankar sabbay chraen!
I want to improve my level in Khmer - khnhom chng keloma kamrit robsakhnhom chea pheasaeakhmer
I want to improve my level in Khmer - khnhom chng keloma kamrit robsakhnhom chea pheasaeakhmer
Do you have time to speak with me? - tae anak mean pel niyeay cheamuoy khnhom te?
Do you have time to speak with me? - tae anak mean pel niyeay cheamuoy khnhom te?
Can you please speak in Khmer? - tae anak ach niyeay chea pheasaeakhmer ban te?
Can you please speak in Khmer? - tae anak ach niyeay chea pheasaeakhmer ban te?
Are things always this difficult in Cambodia? - tae avei tengteman kar lombak nowknong bratesa kampouchea te?

Are things always this difficult in Cambodia? - tae avei tengteman kar lombak nowknong bratesa kampouchea te?
Say hi to him for me - niyeay tha suostei keat samreab khnhom
Say hi to him for me - niyeay tha suostei keat samreab khnhom
Say hi to her for me - niyeay tha suostei neang samreab khnhom
Say hi to her for me - niyeay tha suostei neang samreab khnhom
How did you meet each other? - tae anak ban chuobaknea yeang dauchamtech?
How did you meet each other? - tae anak ban chuobaknea yeang dauchamtech?
What do you want me to do? - te ei anak chng e a y khnhom thve ei avei?
What do you want me to do? - te ei anak chng e a y khnhom thve ei avei?
It makes me emotional - vea thveu aoy khnhom romchuolchet
It makes me emotional - vea thveu aoy khnhom romchuolchet
You make everything difficult - anak thveuaoy avei pibeak
You make everything difficult - anak thveuaoy avei pibeak
You make everything easy - anak thveu avei krobyeang ngeayosruol
You make everything easy - anak thveu avei krobyeang ngeayosruol
It makes me hungry - vea thveu aoy khnhom khlean
It makes me hungry - vea thveu aoy khnhom khlean
Fasten your seat-belts! - dak khsae kr veat kawei aoy luen!
Fasten your seat-belts! - dak khsae kr veat kawei aoy luen!
You look great tonight - anak meul tow aschary now yb nih
You look great tonight - anak meul tow aschary now yb nih
Should I bring the umbrella? - tae khnhom kuor yk chhtr te?
Should I bring the umbrella? - tae khnhom kuor yk chhtr te?
you're crazy - Yap moung

you're crazy - Yap moung

Will you visit us? - tae anak nung mokleng yeung te?
Will you visit us? - tae anak nung mokleng yeung te?
I like singing. - khnhom chaulchett chrieng .
I like singing. - khnhom chaulchett chrieng .
I like cooking - khnhom chaulchett chamain ahar
I like cooking - khnhom chaulchett chamain ahar
I like playing soccer - khnhom chaulchett leng balteat
I like playing soccer - khnhom chaulchett leng balteat
I like listening to music. - khnhom chaulchett stab tantrei .
I like listening to music. - khnhom chaulchett stab tantrei .

I like reading - khnhom chaul chett an
I like reading - khnhom chaul chett an
I like to relax - khnhom chaulchett samreak
I like to relax - khnhom chaulchett samreak
I like dancing. - khnhom chaulchett roam .
I like dancing. - khnhom chaulchett roam .
We are going to play football - yeung nung leng balteat
We are going to play football - yeung nung leng balteat
When are you going swimming? - tae anak heltuk nowpel na?
When are you going swimming? - tae anak heltuk nowpel na?
Only a few people - meante mnoussa pirbei neak bonnaoh
Only a few people - meante mnoussa pirbei neak bonnaoh
He's very rich - keat chea anak mean nasa
He's very rich - keat chea anak mean nasa

I enjoyed myself very much - khnhom pitchea sabbay nasa
I enjoyed myself very much - khnhom pitchea sabbay nasa
I agree with you - khnhom ylsrab tam anak
I agree with you - khnhom ylsrab tam anak
Are you sure? - tae anak brakd te?
Are you sure? - tae anak brakd te?
Be careful! - saum brongobraytn!
Be careful! - saum brongobraytn!
Cheers! - chy yo!
Cheers! - chy yo!
Would you like to go for a walk? - tae anak chng tow daerleng te?
Would you like to go for a walk? - tae anak chng tow daerleng te?
Good luck! - saum saamnangola!
Good luck! - saum saamnangola!
Congratulations! - saum abaarsatr!
Congratulations! - saum abaarsatr!
Enjoy! (before eating) - saum anhcheunh!(moun nhoam ahar)
Enjoy! (before eating) - saum anhcheunh!(moun nhoam ahar)
Bless you (when sneezing) - sbaey(pel kandasa)
Bless you (when sneezing) - sbaey(pel kandasa)
Best wishes! - saumchounopr krobbrakear!
Best wishes! - saumchounopr krobbrakear!
Transportation - kar doekachonhchoun
Transportation - kar doekachonhchoun
It's freezing - vea trachak chng kk
It's freezing - vea trachak chng kk
It's cold - vea trachak
It's cold - vea trachak
It's hot - vea kdaw

It's hot - vea kdaw
So so - sokhasabbay
So so - sokhasabbay
When did this movie start? - gohn nih chab leng Ƅee-ang·kahl
When did this movie start? - gohn nih chab leng Ƅee-ang·kahl
I came yesterday - kuh·nyohm mao Ƅee-muh·suhl-mein
I came yesterday - kuh·nyohm mao Ƅee-muh·suhl-mein
I'm from Japan - khnhom mk pi bratesa chbon
I'm from Japan - khnhom mk pi bratesa chbon
The letter is inside the book - saambotr ku nowknong sievphow
The letter is inside the book - saambotr ku nowknong sievphow
I was born in Miami - khnhom kaet nowknong tikrong mai a mi
I was born in Miami - khnhom kaet nowknong tikrong mai a mi
The pen is under the desk - bich ku now kraom tosarser
The pen is under the desk - bich ku now kraom tosarser
Can I practice Italian with you? - tae khnhom ach anouvott pheasaea aiteali chea muo uo y anak ban te?
Can I practice Italian with you? - tae khnhom ach anouvott pheasaea aiteali chea muo uo y anak ban te?
I speak French but with an accent - khnhom niyeay pheasaea barang minola
I speak French but with an accent - khnhom niyeay pheasaea barang minola
No one here speaks Greek - kmean anaknea now tinih niyeay pheasaea kre chte
No one here speaks Greek - kmean anaknea now tinih niyeay pheasaea kre chte
You should not forget this word - anak min kuor phlech peaky nih te
You should not forget this word - anak min kuor phlech peaky nih te
This is not correct - vea min troemotrauv te
This is not correct - vea min troemotrauv te
I'm not fluent in Italian yet - khnhom niyeay pheasaea aiteali mintean stat te
I'm not fluent in Italian yet - khnhom niyeay pheasaea aiteali mintean stat te
I saw you - khnhom ban chuob anak
I saw you - khnhom ban chuob anak
You played tennis - anak ban leng ten nisa
You played tennis - anak ban leng ten nisa
We thought Spanish is easy - puok yeung kitthea pheasaea esbanh sruol rien
We thought Spanish is easy - puok yeung kitthea pheasaea esbanh sruol rien
They drove a car - puokke ban baeklan
They drove a car - puokke ban baeklan
We wanted to learn - puok yeung chng rien
We wanted to learn - puok yeung chng rien
Who is knocking at the door? - tae norna kampoung kohtvear?
Who is knocking at the door? - tae norna kampoung kohtvear?
When can we meet? - tae pelna yeung ach chuobaknea ban?
When can we meet? - tae pelna yeung ach chuobaknea ban?

Where do you live? - tae anak rsanow tinea?
Where do you live? - tae anak rsanow tinea?
What is your name? - tae anak chhmoh avei?
What is your name? - tae anak chhmoh avei?
Do you know her? - tae anak skal neang ryyte?
Do you know her? - tae anak skal neang ryyte?
I'm just looking around. - Merl leng té
I'm just looking around. - Merl leng té
I think I saw you somewhere - Dorch kernch nov na
I think I saw you somewhere - Dorch kernch nov na
you are wearing a very beautiful dress - Peak ko ail sa-art nas dol huy
you are wearing a very beautiful dress - Peak ko ail sa-art nas dol huy
after your work is done – do you like to go outside and eat something with me? - Pel chop tvwer gar huy dtov nhum ei grao chia moiu bong te?
after your work is done – do you like to go outside and eat something with me? - Pel chop tvwer gar huy dtov nhum ei grao chia moiu bong te?
Can I have your number? - Soam nek dtour-ro-subp ban te?
Can I have your number? - Soam nek dtour-ro-subp ban te?
do you have a boyfriend yet? - Mien song sa nov?
do you have a boyfriend yet? - Mien song sa nov?
your face looks similiar to someone. - Moak neng dorch skorl
your face looks similiar to someone. - Moak neng dorch skorl
Do you have a fiancé? - Dtau nek mian koo-don-deng dtee?
Do you have a fiancé? - Dtau nek mian koo-don-deng dtee?
How is your fiancé? - Koo-don-deng ro-bos nek yang meej del?
How is your fiancé? - Koo-don-deng ro-bos nek yang meej del?
Speak louder. - niyeay aoy khlang .
Speak louder. - niyeay aoy khlang .
Speak slowly. - niyeay yut .
Speak slowly. - niyeay yut .
I'll call back in an hour. - khnhom nung toursapt tralbmokvinh knongorypel muoy maong .
I'll call back in an hour. - khnhom nung toursapt tralbmokvinh knongorypel muoy maong .

<u>If I had some money, I would buy her a gift.</u> - brasenbae khnhom mean louy khleah khnhom nung tinh amnaoy robsa neang .
<u>If I had some money, I would buy her a gift.</u> - brasenbae khnhom mean louy khleah khnhom nung tinh amnaoy robsa neang .
I can't go out tonight because I must study. - khnhom min ach chenhtow kraw now yb nih ban te proh khnhom trauvte seksaa .
I can't go out tonight because I must study. - khnhom min ach chenhtow kraw now yb nih ban te proh khnhom trauvte seksaa .
Where are the nightclubs? - <u>a-e nâ mee-uhn bâ</u>

Where are the nightclubs? - <u>a-e nâ mee-uhn bâ</u>
Don't play the music too loud. - kom lengophleng too khlangpek .
Don't play the music too loud. - kom lengophleng too khlangpek .
Where do you live? - tae anak rsanow ena?
Where do you live? - tae anak rsanow ena?
My house is in Phnom Penh. - phteah khnhom now phnompenh .
My house is in Phnom Penh. - phteah khnhom now phnompenh .
Where do you work? - tae anak thveukear nowenea?
Where do you work? - tae anak thveukear nowenea?
I work at the Ministry of Education. - khnhom thveukear now krasuong abrom .
I work at the Ministry of Education. - khnhom thveukear now krasuong abrom .
Have you been here long? - tae anak now tinih your te?
Have you been here long? - tae anak now tinih your te?
I've been in Cambodia one week. - khnhom ban nowknong bratesa kampouchea muoy sa bta haey .
I've been in Cambodia one week. - khnhom ban nowknong bratesa kampouchea muoy sa bta haey .
Are you enjoying your visit? - tae anak rikreay nung damnaer tossaankechch robsa anak te?
Are you enjoying your visit? - tae anak rikreay nung damnaer tossaankechch robsa anak te?
You speak Khmer very well. - anak niyeay khmer ban la nasa .
You speak Khmer very well. - anak niyeay khmer ban la nasa .
This is a gift for you. - nih kuchea amnaoy samreab anak .
This is a gift for you. - nih kuchea amnaoy samreab anak .
Is there enough petrol in the tank? - tae mean brenginthon krobkrean nowknong thoung der ryyte?
Is there enough petrol in the tank? - tae mean brenginthon krobkrean nowknong thoung der ryyte?

Adjectives

Big - thom
Big - thom
Small - tauch
Small - tauch
Long - veng
Long - veng
Short - khlei
Short - khlei
Tall - khpasa
Tall - khpasa
Thick - krasa

Thick - krasa
Thin - staeng
Thin - staeng
Wide - touleay
Wide - touleay
Bad - akrak / minola
Bad - akrak / minola
Good - la
Good - la
Easy - ngeayosruol
Easy - ngeayosruol
Difficult - pibeak
Difficult - pibeak
Expensive - thlai
Expensive - thlai
Cheap - thaok
Cheap - thaok
Fast - luen
Fast - luen
Slow - yut
Slow - yut
Young - kmeng
Young - kmeng
New - thmei
New - thmei
Heavy - thngon
Heavy - thngon
Empty - tte
Empty - tte
Full - penh
Full - penh
Right - troemotrauv
Right - troemotrauv
Wrong - khosa
Wrong - khosa
Strong - khlang
Strong - khlang
Weak - khsaaoy
Weak - khsaaoy
Sharp - mout
Sharp - mout
Mesmerizing - thveu aoy mean pheaprungmoam
Mesmerizing - thveu aoy mean pheaprungmoam

Near - chit haey
Near - chit haey
True - pit
True - pit
Comfortable - mean pha sokhpheap
Comfortable - mean pha sokhpheap
Common - thommotea
Common - thommotea
Cheap - thaok
Cheap - thaok
Opposite - phtoy
Opposite - phtoy
Delicate - chhnganh
Delicate - chhnganh
Shiny - phlu chang
Shiny - phlu chang
Expensive - thlai nasa
Expensive - thlai nasa
Fresh - srasa

Fresh - srasa

Hollow - brahaong

Hollow - brahaong

Thick - krasa

Thick - krasa

Unbelievable - min kuor aoy chue

Unbelievable - min kuor aoy chue

Remarkable - kuor aoy ktsamkeal

Remarkable - kuor aoy ktsamkeal

Useless - kmean brayoch

Useless - kmean brayoch

False - min pit

False - min pit

Annoying - romkhan

Annoying - romkhan

Comforting - kar luonglom chet

Comforting - kar luonglom chet

Wealthy - tropyosambotte

Wealthy - tropyosambotte
Violent - hoe ngsaea
Violent - hoe ngsaea
Wealthy - tropyosambotte
Wealthy - tropyosambotte
Overwhelmed - huosa kamrit
Overwhelmed - huosa kamrit
Exhausted - htnuey
Exhausted - htnuey
Ripe - toum
Ripe - toum
Traditional - chea brapeinei
Traditional - chea brapeinei
Frustrated - khakchet
Frustrated - khakchet
Is this a new or old book?- tae nih chea sievphow thmei ryy chasa?
Is this a new or old book?- tae nih chea sievphow thmei ryy chasa?
Am I right or wrong? - tae khnhom niyeay trauv ryy khosa?
Am I right or wrong? - tae khnhom niyeay trauv ryy khosa?
Is he younger or older than you? - tae keat kmeng cheang ryy chasa cheang anak?
Is he younger or older than you? - tae keat kmeng cheang ryy chasa cheang anak?
Is the test easy or difficult? - tae kar bralng nih sruol ryy pibeak?
Is the test easy or difficult? - tae kar bralng nih sruol ryy pibeak?
This is very expensive - vea thlai nasa
This is very expensive - vea thlai nasa
Is she tall? - tae neang khpasa te?
Is she tall? - tae neang khpasa te?
Heartbroken - kooik-jet
Heartbroken - kooik-jet
Crazy - chugat
Crazy - chugat
to marry - riab-gaa
to marry - riab-gaa
Married - gaa
Married - gaa
Single - liiw
Single - liiw
steady lover - seong-saa

steady lover - seong-saa
Husband - bdey
Husband - bdey
Wife - bproon-bpon
Wife - bproon-bpon
beautiful girl - srey saart
beautiful girl - srey saart
Beautiful - sa-art
Beautiful - sa-art
Handsome - pro sa-art
Handsome - pro sa-art

Verbs
Abandon - baohbngchaol
Abandon - baohbngchaol
Hug - aob
Hug - aob
Obey - korp bratebatte
Obey - korp bratebatte
Accept - prom ttuol
Accept - prom ttuol
Advise - phtal yobl
Advise - phtal yobl
Rent - chuol
Rent - chuol
Sharpen - mout
Sharpen - mout
Love - snehea
Love - snehea
Scare - banleach
Scare - banleach
Attack - veayobrahear
Attack - veayobrahear
Help - chomnuoy
Help - chomnuoy
Dance - roam
Dance - roam
Drink - phoek
Drink - phoek
Kiss - thaeb
Kiss - thaeb
Regret - saok sta y
Regret - saok sta y

Celebrate - abaarsator
Celebrate - abaarsator
Walk - daer
Walk - daer
Begin - daembi chab phtae m
Begin - daembi chab phtae m
Sing - chrieng
Sing - chrieng
Eat - nhoam
Eat - nhoam
Buy - tinh
Buy - tinh
Communicate - teaktong
Communicate - teaktong
Drive - baekabar
Drive - baekabar
Know - daembi doeng
Know - daembi doeng
Run - rt
Run - rt
Believe - chue
Believe - chue
Decide - samrechchet
Decide - samrechchet
Leave - chakchenh
Leave - chakchenh
Rest - samreak
Rest - samreak
Draw - kour
Draw - kour
Describe - pipnrnea
Describe - pipnrnea
Apologize - som aphytos
Apologize - som aphytos
Sleep - tow keng

Sleep - tow keng
Choose - chreusareus
Choose - chreusareus
Write - sarser
Write - sarser
Listen - stab
Listen - stab
Wait - rngcham
Wait - rngcham
Receive - totoul
Receive - totoul
Give - oy
Give - oy
Forget - plej
Forget - plej
Speak - niyeay
Speak - niyeay

Pronouns and Possessive Pronouns

I - khnhom
I - khnhom
You - nak
You - nak
She - neang
She - neang
He - kat
He - kat
We - yeung
We - yeung
They - pouk ke
They - pouk ke
It - vea
It - vea
my pen - bich robos khnhom
my pen - bich robos khnhom
your cat - chmar robos nak
your cat - chmar robos nak

our book - seavpov robos yeung
our book - seavpov robos yeung
my passport - likhetachchlangden robos khnhom
my passport - likhetachchlangden robos khnhom
his photo - roubathat robos kat
his photo - roubathat robos kat
her seat - kawei robos neang
her seat - kawei robos neang
its price - tamlei robos vea
its price - tamlei robos vea
our plane - yontohaoh robos yeung
our plane - yontohaoh robos yeung
their money - louy robos pouk ke
their money - louy robos pouk ke

Body Parts

Hair - sauk
Hair - sauk
Face - mok
Face - mok
Eye - pnaak
Eye - pnaak
Nose - jrau-moh
Nose - jrau-moh
Mouth - moat
Mouth - moat
Chin - jaung-gaa
Chin - jaung-gaa
Lips - bau-boo-moat
Lips - bau-boo-moat
Teeth - tmeeñ
Teeth - tmeeñ
Ear - dtrau-jiak
Ear - dtrau-jiak
Neck - gau
Neck - gau
Chest - dtruung
Chest - dtruung
Back - knaung
Back - knaung
Stomach - bpuah

Stomach - bpuah
arm or hand - dai
arm or hand - dai
Finger - mriam-dai
Finger - mriam-dai
Shoulder - smaa
Shoulder - smaa
foot or leg - jaung
foot or leg - jaung
Toe - mriam-jaung
Toe - mriam-jaung
Knee - jong-gong
Knee - jong-gong
Thigh - plul
Thigh - plul
Skin - sbaek
Skin - sbaek
Brain - kua-gbaal
Brain - kua-gbaal
Heart - beh-doong
Heart - beh-doong
Lung - suat
Lung - suat
Liver - tlaum
Liver - tlaum

Nature

Cliff - chrang thm chaot

Cliff - chrang thm chaot

Seaweed - sa rea y samout

Seaweed - sa rea y samout

Forest - preichheu

Forest - preichheu

Waterfall - tukachroh

Waterfall - tukachroh

Hill - phnom

Hill - phnom

Tree - daemchheu

Tree - daemchheu

Sky - mekh
Sky - mekh
Sand - khsaach
Sand - khsaach
Mud - phk
Mud - phk
Cave - roungophnom
Cave - roungophnom
Star - phkay
Star - phkay
Desert - vealokhsaach
Desert - vealokhsaach
Wildlife - satvaprei
Wildlife - satvaprei
Glacier - phtang tukakak
Glacier - phtang tukakak
Lake - boeng
Lake - boeng
Grass - smaw
Grass - smaw
Moon - preah chn
Moon - preah chn
Nature - thommocheate
Nature - thommocheate
Cloud - popok
Cloud - popok
Ocean - mhasamout
Ocean - mhasamout
Mountain - phnom
Mountain - phnom
Grass - smaw
Grass - smaw

River - tonle
River - tonle
Jungle - prei
Jungle - prei
Sun - preahatit
Sun - preahatit
Tropical - tambn traupik
Tropical - tambn traupik
Volcano - phnomphleung
Volcano - phnomphleung

27

Celebrations

Wedding - apa pipea
Wedding - apa pipea
Graduation - banhchob karseksaea
Graduation - banhchob karseksaea
Celebration - kar braropth pithi
Celebration - kar braropth pithi
Christmas - bonyanauel
Christmas - bonyanauel
Birthday - thngaikamnaet
Birthday - thngaikamnaet
Bride - kaunokramoum
Bride - kaunokramoum
Groom - kaunkamloh
Groom - kaunkamloh
Easter - bony ai staer
Easter - bony ai staer
Festival - mhaosrap
Festival - mhaosrap
Khmer New Year - bonyachaulochhnam khmer
Khmer New Year - bonyachaulochhnam khmer
Water Festival - pithi bonyaomtouk
Water Festival - pithi bonyaomtouk
Labour Day - tivea polokam
Labour Day - tivea polokam

12

Sports

Baseball - be sb l
Baseball - be sb l
Cycling - chiahkng
Cycling - chiahkng
Badminton - keila veay sei
Badminton - keila veay sei
Basketball - balbaoh
Basketball - balbaoh
Football - balteat
Football - balteat
Gymnastics - anak hat kayosampn
Gymnastics - anak hat kayosampn
Dancing - roam
Dancing - roam
Golf - keila veaykaunkol
Golf - keila veaykaunkol
Skiing - chiah skei
Skiing - chiah skei
Swimming - heltuk

Swimming - heltuk

Hiking - laengophnom

Hiking - laengophnom

Tennis - keila veay kaun bal

Tennis - keila veay kaun bal

Volleyball - balteah

Volleyball - balteah

Professions

Lawyer - metheavi
Lawyer - metheavi
Actor - tara sa mte ng
Actor - tara sa mte ng
Actress - tuo srei
Actress - tuo srei
Farmer - ksekar
Farmer - ksekar
Artist - selbokar
Artist - selbokar
Dancer - anak roam

Dancer - anak roam
Banker - thneakearik
Banker - thneakearik
Librarian - bannarok
Librarian - bannarok
Biologist - chi v vitou
Biologist - chi v vitou
Carpenter - cheangchheu
Carpenter - cheangchheu
Scientist - anak vityea sa sr t
Scientist - anak vityea sa sr t
Cashier - belakar
Cashier - belakar
Astronaut - avkasayeanik
Astronaut - avkasayeanik
Surgeon - kroupety veahkat
Surgeon - kroupety veahkat
Chef - chongphow
Chef - chongphow
Singer - anak chamrieng
Singer - anak chamrieng
Bartender - bu r du r
Bartender - bu r du r
Electrician - cheang akkisa ni
Electrician - cheang akkisa ni
Ambassador - ekaakk rodthatout
Ambassador - ekaakk rodthatout
Dentist - petyothmenh
Dentist - petyothmenh
Nurse - kileanoubadthayikea
Nurse - kileanoubadthayikea
Dermatologist - kroupety chomneanh khang saesbek
Dermatologist - kroupety chomneanh khang saesbek

Designer - anak rochnea
Designer - anak rochnea
Writer - anaknipon
Writer - anaknipon
Manager - anakakrobkrong
Manager - anakakrobkrong
Pharmacist - aosathkari
Pharmacist - aosathkari
Florist - anak lk phka
Florist - anak lk phka
Plumber - cheangkatsak
Plumber - cheangkatsak
Engineer - visvakar
Engineer - visvakar
Gardener - anak the suon
Gardener - anak the suon
Cleaner - anakbaosasaamat
Cleaner - anakbaosasaamat
Teacher - krou
Teacher - krou
Manicurist - mea ni kurist
Manicurist - mea ni kurist
Doctor - vechchobandet
Doctor - vechchobandet
Pediatrician - kroupety komar
Pediatrician - kroupety komar
Hairdresser - cheangkatsak
Hairdresser - cheangkatsak
Journalist - anaksaearptrmean
Journalist - anaksaearptrmean
Pilot - anakbaekayontohaoh
Pilot - anakbaekayontohaoh

Poet - kamnap
Poet - kamnap
Politician - anak nyobeay
Politician - anak nyobeay
Paramedic - kroupet
Paramedic - kroupet
President - brathan
President - brathan
Translator - anakabakabre
Translator - anakabakabre
Receptionist - anakattuol phnhiev
Receptionist - anakattuol phnhiev
clerk - smien
clerk - smien
janitor - anakyeamkouk
janitor - anakyeamkouk
Electrician - cheang akkisa ni
Electrician - cheang akkisa ni

Countries
Cambodia - bratesa kampouchea
Cambodia - bratesa kampouchea
Thailand - thai
Thailand - thai
Vietnam - vietneam
Vietnam - vietneam
Laos - lav
Laos - lav
China - chen
China - chen
Japan - chbon
Japan - chbon
Nepal - nebal
Nepal - nebal
Philippines - hveilipin
Philippines - hveilipin
Malaysia - bratesa mealesai

Malaysia - bratesa mealesai
Myanmar - miyeanmea
Myanmar - miyeanmea
Indonesia - indau ne sai
Indonesia - indau ne sai
Bhutan - bou tan
Bhutan - bou tan
United States - saharodthaamerik
United States - saharodthaamerik
England - bratesa angkles
England - bratesa angkles
New Zealand - nou ve l se lng
New Zealand - nou ve l se lng
Australia - australi
Australia - australi
Singapore - bratesa senghobori
Singapore - bratesa senghobori
Mongolia - mo l lau
Mongolia - mo l lau
New Zealand - nou ve l se lng
New Zealand - nou ve l se lng
South Africa - a prich khangotbaung
South Africa - a prich khangotbaung
Kenya - kenyea
Kenya - kenyea
Egypt - ehsaib
Egypt - ehsaib
Greece - bratesa krek
Greece - bratesa krek
Italy - bratesa aiteali
Italy - bratesa aiteali
Spain - esbanh
Spain - esbanh
Sweden - saouyet

Sweden - saouyet

Norway - nrves

Norway - nrves

Netherlands - hau ll ng

Netherlands - hau ll ng

Continents

America - a me ri ch
America - a me ri ch
Asia - asai

Asia - asai

Europe - eurob

Europe - eurob
Africa - ahvrik

Africa - ahvrik

Oceania - au se a ni

Oceania - au se a ni
Antarctica - angtaktik

Antarctica - angtaktik

At the bank

I'd like to open a bank account. - khnhom chng baek konni thneakear .

I'd like to open a bank account. - khnhom chng baek konni thneakear .

My credit card does not work. - kat intean robsakhnhom min damnaerkar te .

My credit card does not work. - kat intean robsakhnhom min damnaerkar te .

Withdraw money - dk louy

Withdraw money - dk louy

I need a loan. - khnhom trauvkar brakkamchi .

I need a loan. - khnhom trauvkar brakkamchi .

Hairdresser

Do you have an appointment? - tae anak mean karnatchuob te?
Do you have an appointment? - tae anak mean karnatchuob te?

I want to cut my hair short please. - khnhom chng katsak aoy khlei .
I want to cut my hair short please. - khnhom chng katsak aoy khlei .
How would like your haircut? - tae anak chng katsak robsa anak yeang dauchamtech?
How would like your haircut? - tae anak chng katsak robsa anak yeang dauchamtech?

Signs
For sale - samreab lk
For sale - samreab lk
One way - phlauv muoy
One way - phlauv muoy
No smoking - ham chkbari
No smoking - ham chkbari
Train platform - vetikea rothaphleung
Train platform - vetikea rothaphleung
Working days - thngai thveukear
Working days - thngai thveukear
For rent - samreab chuol
For rent - samreab chuol

Driving
Driving - baekabar
Driving - baekabar
Traffic - chreachar
Traffic - chreachar
Road - phlauv
Road - phlauv
pothole - phaengophka
pothole - phaengophka
Collision - bok
Collision - bok
petrol station - stha ni breng i nt
petrol station - stha ni breng i nt
Motorcycle - mautau
Motorcycle - mautau
Tires - saambk kng rothayon
Tires - saambk kng rothayon
Kilometers - kilaumet
Kilometers - kilaumet
stop sign - sanhnhea chhb
stop sign - sanhnhea chhb
The government never fixes the potholes. - rodthaphibeal min del chuosachoul phnaur noh te .

The government never fixes the potholes. - rodthaphibeal min del chuosachoul phnaur noh te .
In Cambodia, the roads are very dangerous. - now bratesa kampouchea phlauvothnal mean krohthnak nasa .
In Cambodia, the roads are very dangerous. - now bratesa kampouchea phlauvothnal mean krohthnak nasa .
If you ride a motorcycle, you must wear a helmet. - brasenbae anak chiah mautau anak trauvte peakmuok sovotthephap .
If you ride a motorcycle, you must wear a helmet. - brasenbae anak chiah mautau anak trauvte peakmuok sovotthephap .
During rainy season, floodwater can fill the streets. - knong rdauvovossaa tukchomnn ach haur penh phlauv .
During rainy season, floodwater can fill the streets. - knong rdauvovossaa tukchomnn ach haur penh phlauv .
It is easy to have a collision. - ngeay nung meankar bahtongkich .
It is easy to have a collision. - ngeay nung meankar bahtongkich .
There is lots of traffic. - mean chreachar chraen .
There is lots of traffic. - mean chreachar chraen .
An attendant will pump your petrol. - anakabamreu mneak nung baum sang robsa anak .
An attendant will pump your petrol. - anakabamreu mneak nung baum sang robsa anak .
They can also fill up your tires with air. - puokke ka ach bampenh saambk kng robsa anak daoy khyal phng der .
They can also fill up your tires with air. - puokke ka ach bampenh saambk kng robsa anak daoy khyal phng der .

Dating Phrases

i am single - khnhom now liv
i am single - khnhom now liv
i have a boyfriend - khnhom mean mitt brosa mneak
i have a boyfriend - khnhom mean mitt brosa mneak
i have a girlfriend - khnhom mean mitt srei mneak
i have a girlfriend - khnhom mean mitt srei mneak
I am married - khnhom riebkear haey
I am married - khnhom riebkear haey
What is your number? - tae lekh robsa anak bonman?
What is your number? - tae lekh robsa anak bonman?
you are beautiful - anak pitchea srasa saat
you are beautiful - anak pitchea srasa saat
I miss you - khnhom nuk anak
I miss you - khnhom nuk anak

Slang Khmer

Hello - Susaday

Hello - Susaday

Bye - Li sin huey

Bye - Li sin huey

how are you? - Soksaby

how are you? - Soksaby

I'm fine - Saysabok

I'm fine - Saysabok

Brother - Bong

Brother - Bong

Aunty - Oum

Aunty - Oum

Uncle - pou

Uncle - pou

Foreigner - Barang

Foreigner - Barang

very delicious - Chhnang nas

very delicious - Chhnang nas

Cheers - Choul mouy

Cheers - Choul mouy

how much? - Man

how much? - Man

you're crazy - Yap moung

you're crazy - Yap moung

Sweetheart - Songsaa

Sweetheart - Songsaa

Stupid - Leng'ee Leng'ern

Stupid - Leng'ee Leng'ern

Despicable beyond words - Aday la chan

Despicable beyond words - Aday la chan

Don't bother - "Kom ey

Don't bother - "Kom ey

Printed in Great Britain
by Amazon